LORD CATHERLOUGH'S NOTEBOOKS

On the flyleaf, the bound notebooks are inscribed 'Catherine King, 1852'. Beneath that is inscribed – and scraped/erased out - 'Bolton King, Chadshunt 1873'. Clearly the book was reclaimed from young Bolton after his departure from Chadshunt after his father's death in 1878.

Also written on the same page is, 'This is one of the many manuscript books from Barrells written out by our Great grandfather Robert Knight, Baron Luxborough & Earl of Catherlough. C.B.K.'[1]

On the opposite page is written 'C.O. Higgon', so Catherine's niece, the family historian, owned it at some stage, after which it probably went to her daughter, Frances Hill, and from her to her cousin, Michael Carden, the present owner.

---

[1] Unfortunately, of these 'many manuscript books from Barrells', noted by Catherine Bolton King, these are the only ones to survive (as far as I know). Catherine Bolton King (1838-1923) was the fourth of the six surviving daughters of Edward Bolton King & Georgiana Knight (Lord Catherlough's granddaughter) and the only one to remain unmarried. She lived with her aunt, Mrs Gooch, at Melbourne Hall in Derbyshire and inherited her fortune at her death in 1874. Latterly she lived in Brompton Square in London. Bolton King (1860-1937) was her much younger half-brother.

Note on the author

Robert Knight, the author of these notebooks, was a member of an established City family. His grandfather had left Warwickshire in the mid-seventeenth century and had built up a comfortable fortune. His father gained notoriety as the cashier of the South Sea Company, who had to flee abroad at the time of the crash in 1720. In 1727, Robert married Henrietta St John, the half-sister of the celebrated Lord Bolingbroke, by whom he had two children. They separated in 1736. After her death in 1756, he married Lady Lequesne, the widow of a City magnate, but they separated four years later. From about 1766 he lived happily with a Warwickshire labourer's daughter, Jane Davis, by whom he had four surviving children. He died, aged 69, in 1772.

Robert has not been well served by history. He was brought up a Tory, and throughout his life remained close to those who had made up the 'Patriot' opposition to Sir Robert Walpole (though his purchase of the Walpole pocket borough of Castle Rising in 1747 from the mistress of Sir Robert's disreputable son caused hostile comment). In 1763, when (already Lord Luxborough) he was raised to an Irish earldom, his supposedly low origins were commented on by some whose own ancestry was hardly 'ancient'. At the same time, the arrival of an Anglo-French officer at his house with a baby he claimed was Lord Catherlough's grandson caused a stir in polite society. In 1770, details of his private life was set out for all to laugh at in the semi-pornographic *Town & Country Magazine*. Despite their close association, he has received only passing mentions in the various lives of his brother-in-law, Lord Bolingbroke. He has featured – not usually to his advantage – in surviving letters (mainly from his first wife's friends). Most recently, his reputation was determinedly rubbished in Jane Brown's life of that first wife - Henrietta Knight, Lady Luxborough.

He is mainly remembered today for the collapse of his first marriage. It's difficult for us today to understand the world of the 1730s when it was possible for a man who suspected his wife of adultery, to send her as a semi-prisoner into the Warwickshire countryside[2].

---

[2] Henrietta's banishment took place only ten years after the death of Sophia Dorothea of Celle, wife of King George I, who had spent more than thirty years in prison after the discovery of her affair with Count Köningsmarck (who was killed). 35 years later, in 1772, her great-granddaughter, the Queen of Denmark, was similarly imprisoned and her lover was also killed.

There were undoubtedly double standards. A wife was expected to turn a blind eye to her husband's infidelities, while a husband who similarly condoned or tolerated his wife's was ridiculed as a cuckold – sometimes in villages forced to ride backwards on a horse wearing the cuckold's horns. Yet neither Robert Knight nor his wife let the crisis of 1736 define their lives. Henrietta is recognised today as more than an errant wife (if that is what she was). But Robert too was more than a vindictive cuckold (if that is what he was).

The Notebooks

Surviving letters show that however unsuccessful he was as a husband, he was a loyal and devoted father to his daughter by his first wife. This was Henrietta Knight, Mrs Wymondesold, later Mrs Child, and later still, according to her father (though improbably), Countess Duroure. She was one of the most notorious ladies of her generation, but her father stuck by her, despite some ridicule, and despite his loyalty to her causing the end of his second marriage. He loved her and she adored him.

The notebooks give us a picture of the man that complements the one we have from his letters. They are undated. The last published source is from the mid-1740s, but the books seem to come from the last years of his life.

There is a calm reflectiveness about the excerpts that would be in keeping with the happiness he found with Jane in his last years. The volume consists of three notebooks that were later bound together. Each has its own different character. The first (pp. 10-52) consists mainly of quotes from Locke and Pope and is the most intellectually demanding of the three.

It begins with extracts from Locke's *Essay Concerning Human Understanding* (1690) and Pope's *Essay on Man* (1732-4). Lord Catherlough is interested by the question that intrigued Locke – what are the limits of the mind in its attempts to understand the world? He seems to accept Locke's insistence on the role of sensory experience (rather than reason) in the accumulation of knowledge. However, Locke's acceptance of the ancient idea of a 'chain of being', from God himself down to the least animate objects in creation, makes space for some interesting speculation on the possibility of there being other beings – 'Spirits' - in the universe with far greater intellectual capacities than ours. Lord Catherlough quotes extensively from these speculations.

Locke, the radical Whig, and Pope, the recusant Tory (with Jacobite sympathies) are often seen as polar opposites, but Lord

Catherlough was interested in their similarities. Bolingbroke himself, who was so close to Pope, owed more to Locke than he was prepared to admit. Locke and Pope shared a sense of the immensity of creation, of man's lowly place in it, and of our need to humble our intellects before the overriding wisdom of God. Lord Catherlough would have known Pope. The *Essay on Man* took the form of a series of letters to Lord Bolingbroke. Pope was a regular visitor during the Dawley years, when Robert Knight (as he then was) and his wife were also often there.

The first book ends with extensive extracts from Dr Thomas Morgan's *Physico-Theology*, published in 1741. Physico-Theology was an eighteenth century term for natural theology, whereby an argument for the existence of God was demonstrated in nature – most usually in seeing an intelligent design. Morgan however, in an earlier work, had linked his arguments to a denial of revelation and of the doctrine of the Trinity, which had set him against his Presbyterian congregation in Marlborough. Presbyterian ministers and/or their congregations often drifted into Unitarianism in the eighteenth century, not least in Clapham (where Lord Catherlough had friends). However, these extracts from the *Physico-*

Theology are not controversial. They echo in large part the extracts from Locke that Lord Catherlough has already copied.

The second notebook (pp.53-92) starts with a number of quotations from Shakespeare. These are generally pearls of wisdom for leading a good life, not unlike the verses from the bible that Lord Catherlough includes in the third book. He continues with Dr Gwithers' book on physiognomy. The relationship of spirit and flesh, mind and body, interested the thinkers of the seventeenth and eighteenth centuries. How was the inner mind revealed in the outer man. By cultivating 'the art of seeing', could we gain a window into men's souls? The notebook ends with Dr Armstrong's best-selling poem on health.

The third notebook (pp.93-204) is double the size of the others and is filled with quotations from the bible – specifically from the books of Ecclesiasticus, the Wisdom of Solomon, Proverbs & Ecclesiastes. All these books focus on a life well lived and are largely lacking in theological content. Like many of his contemporaries, Lord Catherlough was impatient of theology. He wanted moral guidance, and he found it in these four books. They are directed at a comfortably off person, who is probably engaged in business. In short, they were intended for people very much like Lord Catherlough. Nonetheless, despite his avoidance of anything to do with the Fall, or the sacrifice of the cross, he regularly omits passages in Ecclesiasticus that question the idea of an after life, and goes on to quote extensively from the Wisdom of Solomon – a Hellenistic work from around the time of Christ - that strongly agues for it.

Conclusion

It is surprising, considering the dominance of the classics in eighteenth century education, that there are very few quotations from them in this collection. It may be that they were to be found in the now lost books.

Otherwise, the impression gained from this collection is of a thoughtful man, pondering the mysteries of life with considerable humility and openness. It may be that the survival of the first notebook encourages us to believe that Locke and Pope were more important in his thinking than they actually were. Nonetheless, his involvement as a young man with the lively political and intellectual world of Dawley from 1726-1736 must have been important to him, and Locke and Pope were both honoured there. Though a friend of Lord Chesterfield, the is no sense of the 'man of the world philosophy' so much associated with that elegant peer, nor of that secularizing tendency in morals that derive from the writings of the 3rd Earl of Shaftesbury.

Walter King
Chichester, February 2022

Notes on the text

Capitalization was in flux in the eighteenth century, and Lord Catherlough's use of capitals is not consistent. The basic rule had been that nouns were capitalized, and Lord C usually does this. However, he also seems to use capitals when the words have some importance in the sentence. I have tried to capitalize as he does, though with some letters it's difficult to see whether it is intended as a capital or not.

{ } indicates the page numbers in the original manuscript

[ ] indicates words/phrases omitted by Lord Catherlough

[[ ]] indicates words/phrases inserted by Lord Catherlough.

THE FIRST NOTEBOOK

{1} Our Capacity suited to our State – M. Locke[3]
[For] though the Comprehension of our Understandings comes exceeding short of the vast Extent of Things, yet we shall have Cause enough to magnify the Bountiful Author of our being, for that proportion and degree of Knowledge he has bestowed on us, so far above all the rest of the Inhabitants of this our Mansion[4]. Men have Reason to be well satisfied with what God hath thought fit for them, since he hath given them [(as St Peter says) παντα... προς ζωην και ευσεβειαν][5] whatsoever is necessary for the Conveniences of Life and Information of Virtue; and has put within reach of their Discovery , the comfortable provision for this life, and the way that leads to a better. How short soever their Knowledge may come of a universal or perfect Comprehension of whatsoever is, it yet secures their great

---

[3] John Locke, *An Essay Concerning Human Understanding*, 1690 – Book I, Ch. I: Introduction, 5
[4] Lord Catherlough usually capitalizes nouns in his writing – and sometimes other words that he feels have a particular importance. This was a practice that was gradually dying out in his lifetime.
[5] This phrase is omitted by Lord C.

concernments, that they have light enough to lead them to **{2}** the Knowledge of their Maker, and the Sight of their own Duties.

{3} Ideas of God various in different Men. Ch. 4 [§14. Contrary and inconsistent ideas of God under the same name] [6]
Can it be thought that the Ideas men have of God are the Characters and Marks of Himself, engraven on their Minds by his own Finger, when we see that, in the same Country, under one and the same Name, Men have far different, nay often contrary and inconsistent Ideas and Conceptions of Him? Their agreeing in a Name, or a Sound, will scarce prove an innate Notion of him. **[§15. Gross ideas of God]** What true or tolerable notion of a Deity could they have, who acknowledged and worshipped hundreds? Every Deity that they owed above one was infallible evidence of their ignorance of Him, and a proof that they had no true Notion of God, where unity, infinity, and eternity were excluded. To which, if we add their gross Conceptions of Corporeity, **{4}** expressed in their Images and Representations of their

---

[6] John Locke, *An Essay Concerning Human Understanding*, 1690 – Book 1, Ch. 4, *Other considerations concerning Innate Principles,* 13-16. Lord C. takes the title of section 13, but follows it with the text from sections 14 - 16.

Deities, the amours, marriages, copulations, lusts, quarrels, and other mean qualities attributed by them to their gods; we shall have little reason to think, that the heathen world, i.e. the greatest part of mankind, had such ideas of God in their minds, as he himself, out of care that they should not be mistaken about him, was author of......[**§16. Ideas of God not innate]** This was evidently the case of all Gentilism; nor hath even among Jews, Christians, and Mahometans, who acknowledge but one God, this doctrine, and the care taken in those nations to teach men to have true notions of a God, prevailed so far, as to make men to have the same and the true ideas of Him. How many, even among us, will be found, upon inquiry, to fancy him in the shape of a Man sitting in Heaven, **{5}** and to have many other absurd and unfit conceptions of Him? Christians, as well as Turks, have had whole Sects owning and contending earnestly for it, and that the Deity was corporeal, and of Human Shape: [and though we find few among us who profess themselves Anthropomorphites, (though some I have met with that own it)][7] yet, I believe, he that will make it his business, may find, amongst the ignorant and uninstructed Christians, many of that Opinion. Talk but with

---

[7] This phrase is omitted by Lord C.

Country people, almost of any Age, or young people of almost any Condition; and you shall find, that though the name of God be frequently in their Mouths, yet the Notions they apply this name to are so odd, low, and pitiful, that nobody can imagine they were taught by a rational Man, much less that they were Characters writ by the finger of God himself...

{6} M. Locke. Book 2nd, Chap. 10[8]
Nature never makes excellent things for mean or no uses... [9]

...There is a[nother] defect which we may conceive to be in the memory of Man in general, compared with some superior created intellectual Beings, which in this faculty may so far excel Man, that they may have constantly in view the whole scene of all their former actions, wherein no one of the Thoughts they have ever had may slip out of their Sight. The Omniscience of God, who knows all things, past, present, and to come, and to whom the thoughts of Men's hearts always lie open, may satisfy us of the possibility of this. For who can doubt but God may communicate to those Glorious Spirits, **{7}**

---

[8] Book II, Ch. 10: Of Retention, §9

[9] This phrase is actually from Book II, Ch.1: Of Ideas in general, and their Original §15

his immediate Attendants, any of his perfections, in what proportion He pleases, as far as created finite Beings can be capable?

Book 2nd, Chap. 23[10]

[§11] Had we Senses acute enough to discern the minute particles of Bodies, and the real Constitution on which their Sensible Qualities depend, I doubt not but they would produce quite different Ideas in us; and that which is now the yellow Colour of Gold, would then disappear, and instead of it we should see an admirable Texture of parts of a certain Size and Figure. The Microscopes plainly discover to us; for what to our naked Eyes produces a certain Colour, is, by thus But then he would be in augmenting the acuteness of our Senses, discovered to be quite a different thing; **{8}** and the thus altering, as it were, the proportion of the Bulk of the minute parts of a Coloured Object to our usual Sight, produces different ideas from what it did before. Thus Sand or pounded Glass, which is opake, and white to the naked Eye, is pellucid in a Microsope; and a Hair seen this way, loses its former Colour, and is in a great measure pellucid, with a mixture of

---

[10] Book II, Ch. 23: Of our complex Ideas of Substances, §11-12

some bright sparkling Colours, such as appear from the Refraction of Diamonds, and other pellucid Bodies. Blood to the naked Eye appeared all Red; but by a good Microscope, wherein its lesser parts appear, shows only some few Globules of Red, swimming in a pellucid liquor: **{9}** and how these red Globules would appear, if Glasses could be found that could yet magnify them 1000 or 10,000 times more, is uncertain.

[§12] The Infinite[ly] wise Contriver of us, and all things about us, hath fitted our Senses, Faculties, and Organs, to the Conveniences of Life, and the Business we have to do her. We are able, by our Senses, to know and distinguish things; and to examine them so far, as to apply them to our Uses, and several ways to accommodate the Exigencies of [this] Life. We have insight enough into their admirable Contrivances and wonderful Effects, to admire and magnify the Wisdom, power, and Goodness of their Author. Such a Knowledge as this, **{10}** which is suited to our present condition, we want not Faculties to attain. But it appears not, that God intended we should have a perfect, clear, and adequate Knowledge of them: [that perhaps is not in the comprehension of any finite being.] We are furnished with faculties (dull and weak as they are) to discover enough in the Creatures, to lead us to the Knowledge of the Creator, and the Knowledge of our Duty: and we are fitted well enough with Abilities to provide for the conveniences of Living: these are our Business in this World. But were our Senses altered, and made much quicker and acuter, the appearance and outward Scheme of Things would have quite another Face to us; **{11}** and, I am apt to think, would be inconsistent with our Being, or at least Well-being, in this part of the Universe [[or Globe]] which we inhabit. He that considers how little our Constitution is able to bear a Remove into parts of this Air, not much higher than we commonly breathe in, will have Reason to be satisfied, that in this [[part or]] Globe of Earth allotted for our Mansion, the Allwise Architect has suited our Organs, and the Bodies that are to affect them, one to another. If our Sense of Hearing were but 1000 times quicker than it is, how would a perpetual noise distract us? And we should in the quietest Retirement **{12}** be less able to sleep or meditate, than in the middle of a sea-fight. Nay, if that most instructive of our Senses, Seeing, were in any Man a 1000 or a 100,000 times more acute than it is by the best Microscope, things several million times less than the smallest Object of his

Sight now, would then be visible to his naked Eyes, and so he would come nearer [to] the Discovery of the Texture and Motion of the minute parts of Corporeal things; and in many of them, probably get Ideas of their internal Constitutions. **{13}** But then he would be in a quite different world from other people: nothing would appear the same to him, and others; the visible idea of everything would be different. [So that I doubt, whether he and the rest of men could discourse concerning the objects of sight, or have any communication about colours, their appearance being so wholly different.] And perhaps such a Quickness and tenderness of Sight could not endure bright Sun-shine, or so much as open day-light; nor take in but a very small part of any Object at once, and that too only at a very near Distance. And if by the help of such Microscopical Eyes (if I may so call them) a Man could penetrate farther than Ordinary into the Secret Composition and radical Texture of Bodies, he would not make any great **{14}** advantage by the Change, if such an Acute Sight could not serve to conduct him to the Market or Exchange; if he could not see things he was to avoid, at a convenient distance; nor distinguish things he had to do with by those sensible qualities others do. He that was sharp-sighted enough to see the Configuration of the minute particles of the Spring of the Clock, and observe upon what peculiar Structure and Impulse its elastic Motion depends, would no doubt discover something very admirable: but if eyes so framed could not view at once the hand, and the characters if the hour-plate, and thereby at a distance see what o'clock it was, their owner could not be much befitted **{15}** by that acuteness; which, whilst it discovered the secret contrivance of the parts of the machine, made him lose its use.

The bliss of Man (cou'd pride that blessing find)
Is not to act or think beyond Mankind;
No pow'rs of Body or of Soul to share,
But what his Nature and his State can bear.
Why has not Man a Microscopic Eye?
For this plain reason, Man is not a Fly.
Say what the use, were finer optics giv'n,
T' inspect a Mite, not comprehend the Heav'n?
Or touch, if tremblingly alive all o'er,
To smart and agonize at ev'ry pore?
Or keen Effluvia darting thro' the brain,
Die of a rose in aromatic pain?
If nature thunder'd in his opening ears,

And stunn'd him with the Music of the Spheres,

{16} *That to possess any of the sensitive faculties in a higher degree would make Man miserable.*[11]

How would he wish that Heav'n had left him still
The whisp'ring Zephyr, and the purling rill?
Who finds not Providence all good and wise,
Alike in what it gives, and what denies?
Mr Pope[12]

In human works, though labour'd on with pain,
A thousand Movements scarce one purpose gain;
In God's, one single can its End produce;
Yet serves to second too some other use.
So Man, who here seems principal alone,
Perhaps acts second to some Sphere unknown,
Touches some wheel, or verges to some goal;
'Tis but a part we see, and not a whole.[13]

---

[11] These seems to be Lord C's own summaries (at the top of pp. 16-17) of the thesis put forward by Locke, and rendered into verse by Pope.
[12] Alexander Pope, *Essay on Man (to Henry St John, Viscount Bolingbroke)*, Epistle I: VI, 1732-4.
[13] Alexander Pope, *Essay on Man (to Henry St John, Viscount Bolingbroke)*, Epistle I:II, 1732-4

{17} *That throughout the whole visible world an universal order, and gradation is observed.*

Of Systems possible, if 'tis confest
That Wisdom infinite must form the best,
Where all must full or not coherent be,
And all that rises, rise in due degree;
Then, in the Scale of [reas'ning] life [[and sense]], 'tis plain
There must be, somewhere, such a rank as Man:[14]

Far as Creation's ample range extends,
The Scale of Sensual, mental pow'rs ascends:
Mark how it mounts, to Man's imperial race,
From the green myriads in the peopled grass:
What modes of Sight betwixt each wide extreme,
The Mole's dim curtain, and the Lynx's beam:
Of Smell, the headlong Lioness between,
And Hound sagacious on the tainted green:
Of Hearing, from the Life that fills the flood,
To that which warbles through the vernal wood:
{18}[15] The Spider's touch, how exquisitely fine!

---

[14] Alexander Pope, *Essay on Man (to Henry St John, Viscount Bolingbroke)*, Epistle I:II, 1732-4

[15] Lord C gives his own heading across pp. 18-19 –

Feels at each thread, and lives along the line:
In the nice bee, what sense so subtly true
From pois'nous herbs extracts the healing dew:
How Instinct varies in the Grov'lling Swine,
Compar'd, half-reas'ning Elephant, with thine:
'Twixt that, and Reason, what a nice barrier;
For ever sep'rate, yet for ever near!
Remembrance and Reflection how ally'd;
What thin partitions Sense from Thought divide:
And middle natures, how they long to join,
Yet never pass th' insuperable line![16]

See, through this air, this ocean, and this earth,
All matter quick, and bursting into birth.
Above, how high, progressive life may go!
Around, how wide! how deep extend below!
Vast chain of being, which from God began[17],
{19} Natures ethereal, human, angel, man,
Beast, bird, fish, insect! what no eye can see,
No glass can reach! from infinite to thee,

'M. Pope, Epistle 1st, the Gradations of Sense, Instincts, thought, Reason etc.'

[16] Alexander Pope, *Essay on Man (to Henry St John, Viscount Bolingbroke)*, Epistle I:VII, 1732-4

[17] Lord C has noted here 'See M. Locke page 33 upon the same subject' – the idea of a 'great chain of being' was very ancient and remained influential into the nineteenth century.

From thee to nothing![18]

And, if each System in gradation roll
Alike essential to th' amazing Whole,
The least confusion but in one, not all
That System only, but the whole must fall.
Let Earth unbalanc'd from her Orbit fly,
Planets and Suns run lawless through the Sky;
Let ruling Angels from their spheres be hurl'd,
Being on Being wreck'd, and world on world;
Heav'n's whole foundations to their Centre nod,
And Nature tremble to the throne of God.[19]

{20}[20] All are but parts of one stupendous whole,
Whose Body Nature is, and God the Soul;
That, chang'd through all, and yet in all the same,
Great in the Earth, as in th' ethereal frame,
Warms in the Sun, refreshes in the Breeze,
Glows in the Stars, and blossoms in the Trees,

---

[18] Alexander Pope, *Essay on Man (to Henry St John, Viscount Bolingbroke),* Epistle I:VIII, 1732-4. Lord C. notes here, 'to page 30 M Locke'

[19] Alexander Pope, *Essay on Man (to Henry St John, Viscount Bolingbroke),* Epistle I:VIII, 1732-4

[20] Lord C gives his own heading across pp. 20-21, M. Pope, the Absolute Submission due to providence, both as to our present and Future State.

Lives through all Life, extends through all extent,
Spreads undivided, operates unspent,
Breathes in our Soul, informs our mortal part,
As full, as perfect, in a hair as heart;
As full, as perfect, in vile Man that mourns,
As the rapt Seraph that [sings] and burns;
To Him no high, no low, no great, no small;
He fills, he bounds, connects, and equals all.[21]

{21} Know thy own point: This kind, this due degree
Of blindness, weakness, Heav'n bestows on thee.
Submit.—In this, or any other sphere,
Secure to be as blest as thou canst bear:
Safe in the hand of one disposing pow'r,
Or in the natal, or the mortal hour.
All Nature is but Art, unknown to thee;
All Chance, Direction, which thou canst not see;
All Discord, Harmony, not understood;
All partial Evil, universal Good:
And, spite of pride, in erring Reason's spite,
One truth is clear, Whatever is, is Right.[22]

Hope humbly then; with trembling pinions soar;
Wait the great teacher Death; and God adore![23]

---

[21] Alexander Pope, *Essay on Man (to Henry St John, Viscount Bolingbroke*), Epistle I:IX, 1732-4.
[22] Alexander Pope, *Essay on Man (to Henry St John, Viscount Bolingbroke*), Epistle I:X, 1732-4

{22} Blank

{23}[24] Conjecture about Spirits

§ 13. And here give me leave to propose an extravagant Conjecture of mine, viz. That since we have some Reason (if there be any credit to be given to the Report of things, that our philosophy cannot account for) to imagine, that Spirits can assume to themselves Bodies of different Bulk, Figure, and conformation of parts; whether one great advantage some of them have over us, may not lie in this, that they can so frame and shape to themselves Organs of Sensation or perception, as to suit them to their present Design, and the Circumstances of the Object they would consider. For how much would that Man exceed all others in Knowledge, who had but the Faculty so to alter the Structure of his Eyes, **{24}** that one Sense, as to make it capable of all the several degrees of Vision which the assistance of Glasses (casually

---

[23] Alexander Pope, *Essay on Man (to Henry St John, Viscount Bolingbroke*), Epistle I:III, 1732-4. Lord C. ends these excerpts from the first epistle with two lines from the beginning of the epistle, which sum up, for him, the message of the whole.

[24] p.22 is blank. John Locke, *An Essay Concerning Human Understanding*, 1690 Book II:XXIII, 1732-4. Of our complex Ideas of Substances.

at first lighted on) has taught us to conceive? What wonders would he discover, who could so fit his Eye[s] to all sorts of objects, as to see, when he pleased, the Figure and Motion of the minute particles in the Blood, and other Juices of Animals, as distinctly as he does, at other times, the Shape and Motion of the Animals themselves? But to us, in our present State, unalterable Organs so contrived, as to discover the Figure and Motion of the minute parts of **{25}** Bodies, whereon depend those sensible Qualities we now observe in them, would perhaps be of no advantage. God has, no doubt, made them so, as is best for us in our present Condition. He has fitted us for the Neighbourhood of the Bodies that surround us, and we have to do with: And though we cannot, by the Faculties we have, attain to a perfect Knowledge of Things, yet they will serve us well enough for those Ends above-mentioned, which are our great Concernment.

{26} M. Locke, Book 2[d], Chap, 27
[§23] **Consciousness alone makes self**
Nothing but Consciousness can unite remote Existences into the same person, the Identity of Substance will not do it. For whatever Substance there is, however framed, without consciousness there is no person:

{27} [§12] [Whereof] There are probably numberless [[Species of Spirits]]

Book 3[d], Chap. 6

[§11] [For] the Mind..... can have no other notion of Spirit, but by attributing all those Operations, it finds in itself, to a sort of Beings, without consideration of Matter. And even the most advanced Notion we have of God is but attributing... those simple Ideas to Him in an unlimited Degree.... And though we are told, that there are different Species of Angels; yet we know not how to frame distinct specific Ideas of them; not out of any conceit that the Existence of more Species than one of Spirits is impossible, but because having no more simple Ideas (nor being able to frame more) applicable to such Beings, but only those few taken from ourselves, and from the actions of **{28}** our own minds in thinking, and being delighted, and moving several parts of our Bodies, we can no otherwise distinguish in our Conceptions the several Species [of spirits] one from another, but by attributing those Operations and powers, we find in ourselves, to them in a higher or lower degree...

Nor as I [humbly] conceive do we, between God and them in our Ideas, put any difference by any number of simple Ideas, which we have of one, and not of the other, but only that of Infinity. All the particular Ideas of Existence, Knowledge, Will, power, and Motion, &c. being Ideas derived from the Operations of our Minds, we attribute all of them to all **{29}** sorts of Spirits, with the difference only of degrees, to the utmost we can imagine, even Infinity, when we would frame, as well as we can, an Idea of the first Being; who yet, it is certain, is infinitely more remote, in the real Excellency of his Nature, from the highest and perfectest of all created Beings, than the greatest Man, nay purest Seraph[[im]], is from the most contemptible part of Matter; and consequently must infinitely exceed what our narrow understandings can conceive of Him.

{30} Book 3[d] Chap. 6 [§12] **.... in all the visible corporeal world, we see no Chasms or Gaps...** It is not impossible to conceive, nor repugnant to reason, that there may be many Species of Spirits, as much separated and diversified one from another by distinct properties whereof we have no Ideas, as the Species of sensible Things are distinguished one from another by Qualities which we know, and observe in Them.

That there should be more species of Intelligent Creatures above us, than there are of sensible and material below us, is probable to me from hence;

that in all the visible corporeal world, we see no Chasms or Gaps. All quite down from us the Descent is by easy steps, and a continued Series of Things, that in each remove differ very little **{31}** one from the other. There are Fishes that have wings, and are not Strangers to the Airy Region;

and there are some Birds that are Inhabitants of the Water, whose Blood is cold as Fishes, and their Flesh so like in Taste, that the Scrupulous are allowed them on fish-days.

There are animals so near of Kin both to Birds and Beasts, that they are in the middle between both: Amphibious Animals link the Terrestrial and Aquatique together; Seals live at Land and Sea, and porpoises have the warm Blood and Entrails of a Hog, [not to mention what is confidently reported of mermaids or sea-men][25].

{32} M.Locke [Book III;VI §12] **... All quite down from us the descent is by easy steps..**[26]

---

[25] This phrase has been edited out by Lord C.!
[26] Lord C notes 'M. Pope upon the same subject, p. 18.'

There are some Brutes, that seem to have as much Knowledge and Reason, as some that are called Men: and the animal and vegetable Kingdoms are so nearly joined, that if you will take the lowest of one, and the highest of the other, there will scarce be perceived any great difference between them; [[and the polypus lately discovered is found to be both an animal and a vegetable]][27] and so on, till we come to the lowest and the most inorganical parts of Matter, we shall find every-where, that the several Species are linked together, and differ but in almost insensible degrees. **{33}** And when we consider the Infinite power and Wisdom of the Maker, we have reason to think, that it is suitable to the Magnificent Harmony of the

---

[27] This is Lord C's own interpolation into Locke's text. The idea that the natural order could be divided into three kingdoms – the animal, the vegetable and the mineral – was very ancient, but the boundaries of these kingdoms was far from settled. In the eighteenth century, enormous numbers of unknown plants and animals were being discovered and had to be allocated according to their respective kingdom. In 1741, the Swiss naturalist Abraham Trembley (1710-84) discovered the extraordinary regenerative powers of polyps. Plants were known to regenerate from cuttings, but no animal was known to have such power. So was the polyps an animal or a plant? Or was there actually no boundary between them?

Universe, and the great Design and infinite Goodness of the Architect, that the Species of Creatures should also, by gentle Degrees, ascend upward from us toward his infinite perfection, as we see they gradually descend from us downwards: which if it be probable, we have reason then to be persuaded, that there are far more species of Creatures above us, than there are beneath: we being, in degrees of perfection, much more remote from the Infinite being of God, than we are from the lowest state of Being, and that which approaches nearest to nothing.

{35}[28] M. Locke Chap 3^{d}, Book IV[29]

§6 Tis past controversy, that we have in us something that Thinks; our very Doubts about what it is confirm the certainty of its being, though we must content ourselves in the Ignorance of what kind of Being it is: and tis in vain to go about to be Sceptical in this, as it is unreasonable in most other Cases to be positive

---

[28] p. 34 is blank

[29] John Locke, *An Essay Concerning Human Understanding*, 1690: Book IV, *Of Knowledge and Probability,* Chapter III: *Of the Extent of Human Knowledge*, § 6 *Our knowledge, therefore, narrower than our ideas.*

against the being of any thing, because we cannot comprehend its Nature.

For I would fain know what Substance exists, that has not something in it which manifestly baffles our understandings. Other Spirits, who see and know the Nature and inward Constitution of Things, how much must they exceed us in Knowledge? **{36}** To which if we add larger Comprehension, which enables them at one Glance to see the Connexion and agreement of very many Ideas, and readily supplies to them the intermediate proofs, which we by single and slow steps, and long poring in the dark, hardly at last find out, and are often ready to forget one before we have hunted out another: we may guess at some part of the Happiness of Superior Ranks of Spirits, who have a quicker and more penetrating sight, as well as a larger Field of Knowledge.

{37} ...Man is not to be deem'd Imperfect but a Being suited to his place and Rank in the Creation... Pope Ep 1st, verse 20.[30]
Say first, of God above, or Man below,

---

[30] Alexander Pope, *Essay on Man (to Henry St John, Viscount Bolingbroke*), Epistle I, Of the Nature and State of MAN, with respect to the Universe, Introduction.

What can we reason, but from what we know?
Of Man what see we, but his Station here,
From which to reason, or to which refer?
Thro' worlds unnumber'd tho' the God be known,
'Tis ours to trace him only in our own.
He, who thro' vast Immensity can pierce,
See Worlds on Worlds compose one Universe,
Observe how System into System runs,
What other planets and what other Suns,
What varied Being peoples ev'ry Star,
May tell why Heav'n has made us as we are.
But of this Frame the bearings, and the Ties,
The strong connections, nice dependencies,
Gradations just, has thy pervading Soul
Look'd through? or can a part contain the Whole?

{38} M.Locke, Book 4 Chap. 3^d [31]

§ 17. If we are at a loss in respect of the powers and Operations of Bodies, I think it is easy to conclude, we are much more in the dark in reference to the Spirits; whereof we naturally have no Ideas, but what we draw from that of

---

[31] John Locke, *An Essay Concerning Human Understanding*, 1690: Book IV, *Of Knowledge and Probability,* Chapter III: *Of the Extent of Human Knowledge*, §17 Of spirits, yet narrower.

our own, by reflecting on the Operations of our own Souls within us, as far as they can come within our Observation. But how inconsiderable a Rank the Spirits that inhabit our Bodies hold amongst those various and possibly innumerable kinds of Nobler Beings; and how far short they come of the Endowments and perfections of Cherubims and Seraphims, and infinite sorts of Spirits above us; [[has been already]] offered to [[the]] Reader's consideration[32].

{39} Morality capable of Demonstration, Book 4th , Chap 3d [33]

The Idea of a Supreme Being, infinite in power, Goodness, and Wisdom, whose Workmanship we are, and on whom we depend;

and the Idea of ourselves, as understanding Rational Beings; being such as are clear in us, would, I suppose, if duly considered and pursued, afford such Foundations of our Duty and Rules of Action, as might place Morality amongst the Sciences capable of

---

[32]Lord C replaced the original text '...is what by a transient hint, in another place, I have...' He also wrote 'the' instead of Locke's 'my'.

[33] John Locke, *An Essay Concerning Human Understanding*, 1690: Book IV, *Of Knowledge and Probability,* Chapter III: *Of the Extent of Human Knowledge*, §18

Demonstration; wherein I doubt not but from self-evident propositions, by necessary Consequences, as incontestable as those in Mathematics, the Measures of Right and Wrong might be made out **{40}** to any one that will apply himself with the same Indifferency and Attention to the one, as he does to the other of these Sciences.

The Relation of other Modes may certainly be perceived, as well as those of Number and Extension: and I cannot see why they should not also be capable of Demonstration, if due Methods were thought on to examine or pursue their agreement or disagreement.

'Where there is no property, there is no Injustice',

is a proposition as certain as any demonstration in Euclid: for the Idea of property being a right to any thing; and the Idea to which the name Injustice is given, being the Invasion or Violation of that Right; it is evident, that these Ideas, being **{41}** thus established, and these names annexed to them, I can as certainly know this proposition to be true, as that a Triangle has three angles equal to two right ones.

Again, "no Government allows absolute Liberty:"

The Idea of Government being the establishment of Society upon certain Rules or Laws which require Conformity to them; and the Idea of absolute Liberty being for any one to do whatever he pleases; I am as capable of being certain of the Truth of this proposition, as of any in the Mathematics.

{42} M. Locke. Book 4th Chap 3d
[§19] Two things have made Moral Ideas thought uncapable of Demonstration: Their Complexedness, and want of Sensible Representations.

[§20] Remedies of those Difficulties
One part of these Disadvantages in Moral Ideas, which has made them be thought not capable of Demonstration, may in a good measure be remedied by Definitions, setting down that Collection of simple Ideas, which every Term shall stand for, and then using the Terms steadily and constantly for that precise Collection. And what methods Algebra, or something of that kind, may **{43}** hereafter suggest, to remove the other difficulties, it is not easy to foretel. Confident I am, that if Men would, in the same Method, and with the same indifferency, search after Moral, as they do Mathematical Truths, they would find them

have a stronger Connexion one with another, and a more necessary Consequence from our clear and distinct Ideas, and to come nearer perfect Demonstration than is commonly imagined.

But much of this is not to be expected, whilst the desire of Esteem, Riches, or power, makes Men espouse the well-endowed Opinions in Fashion, and then seek Arguments either to make good their Beauty, or varnish over and cover their Deformity: **{44}** Nothing being so beautiful to the Eye, as Truth is to the Mind; nothing so deformed and irreconcileable to the Understanding as a Lye. For tho' many a Man can with satisfaction enough own a no very handsome Wife in his Bosom; yet who is bold enough openly to avow, that he has espoused a Falsehood, and received into his Breast so ugly a thing [as a lye]? Whilst the parties of Men cram their Tenets down all Men's throats, whom they can get into their power, without permitting them to examine their Truth or Falsehood, and will not let Truth have fair play in the World, nor Men the Liberty to search after it; What improvements can be expected of this Kind? What greater Light can **{45}** be hoped for in the Moral Sciences? The subject part of Mankind in most places might, instead thereof, with Egyptian Bondage expect Egyptian

Darkness, were not the Candle of the Lord set up by himself in Men's Minds, which it is impossible for the Breath or power of Man wholly to extinguish.

[§22] Our Ignorance great.
He that knows any thing, knows this in the first place, that he need not seek long for Instances of his Ignorance. The meanest and most obvious Things that come in our way, have dark sides, that the quickest Sight cannot penetrate into. The clearest and most enlarged understanding of thinking men {46} find themselves puzzled, and at a loss, in every particle of Matter, [[from the following causes]]:[34]

1. Want of Ideas.

2. Want of a discoverable Connexion between the Ideas we have.

3d Want of Tracing and examining our Ideas.

---

[34] Lord C place the phrase in double square brackets in stead of the following 'We shall the less wonder to find it so, when we consider the causes of our ignorance; which, from what has been said, I suppose, will be found to be these three:'

{47} [§23] First, there are some things, and those not a few, that we are ignorant of, for want of ideas

[First;] all the Simple Ideas we have, are confined (as I have shown) to those we receive from Corporeal Objects by Sensation, and from the Operations of our own Minds as the Objects of Reflection.

But how much these few and narrow Inlets are disproportionate to the vast whole Extent of all Beings, will not be hard to persuade those, who are not so foolish as to think their Span the Measure of all Things.

What other Simple Ideas tis possible the Creatures in other parts of [[of this Globe or]] [the] universe may have, by the Assistance of Senses and faculties more, or perfecter, than we have, or different from Ours, it is not for us to determine. **{48}** But to say, or think there are no such, because we conceive nothing of them, is no better an argument, than if a Blind Man should be positive in it, that there was no such thing as Light and Colours, because he had no manner of Idea of any such thing, nor could by any means frame to himself any Notions about Seeing.

The Ignorance and Darkness that is in us, no more hinders nor confines the Knowledge that is in Others, than the blindness of a Mole is an Argument against the quick-sightedness of an Eagle.

He that will consider the infinite power, Wisdom, and Goodness of the Creator **{49}** of all Things, will find Reason to think it was not all laid out upon so inconsiderable, mean, and impotent a Creature as he will find Man to be; who, in all probability, is one of the lowest of all Intellectual Beings.

What Faculties therefore other Species of Creatures have, to penetrate into the Nature and inmost Constitutions of Things; what Ideas they may receive of them, far different from Ours; we know not. This we know, and certainly find, that we want several other views of them, besides those we have, to make discoveries of them more perfect. And we may be convinced that the Ideas we can attain to by our Faculties, are very disproportionate...

{50} [§26] Hence no Science of Bodies. [§27] Much less of Spirits Book 4, Chap. 3

...to Things themselves, when a positive, clear, distinct one of Substance itself, which is the Foundation of all the rest, is concealed from us. But want of Ideas of this kind being a part, as well as Cause of our Ignorance, cannot be described.

Only this, I think, I may confidently say of it, that the Intellectual and Sensible world are in this perfectly alike; That that part, which we see of either of them, holds no proportion with what we see not; And whatsoever we can reach with our Eyes, or our Thoughts, of either of them, is but a point, almost nothing in comparison with the rest.

{51} [§22] He that knows any thing, knows this in the first place, that he need not seek long for Instances of his Ignorance. The meanest and most obvious Things that come in our way, have dark sides, that the quickest Sight cannot penetrate into. The clearest and most enlarged Understandings of thinking Men find themselves puzzled, and at a loss, in every particle of Matter.35

[§24] When we consider the vast distance of the known and visible parts of the World, and the Reasons we have to think, that what lies within our Ken is but a small part of the [[immense]] Universe, we shall then discover an

---

[35] It's not clear why Lord C transcribes this paragraph again.

huge Abyss of Ignorance. **{52}** What are the particular Fabrics of the great Masses of Matter, which make up the whole Stupendous frame of Corporeal Beings,

how far they are extended,

what is their motion, and how continued or communicated, and what Influence they have one upon another, are Contemplations that at first glimpse our Thoughts lose themselves in.

If we narrow our Contemplations, and confine our Thoughts to this little Canton, I mean this System of our Sun, and the grosser Masses of Matter, that visibly move about it; what several sorts of Vegetables, Animals, and Intellectual Corporeal Beings, infinitely **{53}** different from those of our little spot of Earth, may there probably be in the other planets, to the Knowledge of which, even of their outward Figures and parts, we can no way attain, whilst we are confined to this earth; there being no natural Means, either by Sensation or Reflection, to convey their Certain ideas into our Minds? They are out of the reach of those Inlets of all our Knowledge: and what sorts of Furniture and Inhabitants those Mansions contain in them, we cannot so much as guess, much less have clear and distinct Ideas of them.

M Locke Book 4. Chap. 3^d [§26] No Science of Bodies [§27] Much Less of Spirits

{54} [§27] To which if we add the Consideration of that infinite Number of Spirits that may be and probably are, which are yet more remote from our Knowledge, whereof we have no cognizance, nor can frame to ourselves any distinct Ideas of their several Ranks and sorts, we shall find this cause of Ignorance conceal from us, in an impenetrable obscurity, almost the whole Intellectual world; a greater certainly, and more beautiful World than the Material. **{55}** [For] bating some very few, and those, if I may so call them, superficial Ideas of Spirit, which by reflection we get of our own, and from thence the best we can collect of the Father of all Spirits, the eternal independent Author of them and us and all Things; we have no certain information, so much as of the Existence of other spirits, but by Revelation.

Angels of all sorts are naturally beyond our discovery: and all those Intelligences whereof it is likely there are more Orders than of Corporeal Substances, are Things whereof our natural Faculties give us no certain account at all.

{56} M. Locke, Book 4, Chap. 6 [Of the Names of Substances]
[§11] [The Qualities which make] Our Complex Ideas of Substances depend [mostly] on [external], remote and unperceivable[36] Causes

But we are so far from being admitted into the Secrets of Nature, that we scarce so much as ever approach the first Entrance towards them. For we are wont to consider the Substances we meet with, each of them, as an entire thing by itself, having all its Qualities in itself, and independent of other things; overlooking, for the most part, the Operations of those invisible Fluids they are encompassed with, and upon whose motions and Operations depend the greatest part of those Qualities which are taken Notice of in them, and are made by us the inherent Marks of distinction whereby we know and denominate them. **{57}**Put a piece of Gold any where by itself, separate from the Reach and Influence of all other Bodies, it will immediately lose all its Colour and Weight, and perhaps Malleableness too; which, for aught I know, would be changed into a perfect Friability. Water, in which to us Fluidity is an Essential Quality, left to itself, would cease to be fluid. But if inanimate Bodies owe so much of their present state to other Bodies without

---

[36] Locke has 'unperceived'

them, that they would not be what they appear to us were those Bodies that environ them removed; it is yet more so in Vegetables, which are nourished, grow, and produce Leaves, Flowers, and Seeds, in a constant Succession. **{58}** And if we look a little nearer into the State of Animals, we shall find that their Dependence, as to Life, Motion, and the most considerable Qualities to be observed in them, is so wholly on extrinsical Causes and Qualities of other Bodies that make no part of them, that they cannot subsist a Moment without them: [though yet those bodies on which they depend are little taken notice of, and make no part of the complex ideas we frame of those animals.]

Take the Air but for a Minute from the greatest part of Living Creatures, and they presently lose Sense, Life, and Motion. This the necessity of Breathing has forced into our Knowledge. But how many other extrinsical and possibly very remote Bodies do the Springs of these admirable Machines depend on, which are not vulgarly observed, or so much as **{59}** thought on; and how many are there which the severest Enquiry can never discover? The Inhabitants of this Spot of the universe, though removed so many Millions of Miles from the sun, yet depend so much on the duly tempered Motion of particles coming from or agitated by it, that were this Earth removed but a small part of the distance out of its present Situation, and placed a little further or nearer that Source of Heat, it is more than probable that the greatest part of the Animals in it would immediately perish: since we find them so often destroyed by an Excess or Defect of the Sun's warmth, which an accidental position in some parts of this our little Globe exposes them to....

{60} ....We see and perceive some of the Motions and grosser Operations of Things here about us; but whence the Streams come that keep all these curious Machines in Motion and Repair, how conveyed and Modified, is beyond our Notice and Apprehension: and the great parts and wheels, as I may so say, of this Stupendous Structure of the Universe, may, for aught we know, have such a connexion and dependence in their Influences and Operations one upon another, that perhaps Things in this our Mansion would put on quite another Face, and cease to be what they are, if some one of the **{61}** Stars or great Bodies incomprehensibly remote from us, should cease to be or move as it does. See page 19 M.Pope

.....nor think tho' Men were none

That Heav'n would want spectators, God want praise;
Millions of Spiritual Creatures walk the Earth
Unseen, both when we wake, and when we Sleep:
All these with ceaseless praise his Works behold
Both Day and Night, Milton[37]

I am apt to join in Opinion with those who believe that all the Regions of Nature swarm with Spirits; and that we have Multitudes of Spectators on all our Actions, when we think our selves most alone: Spectator[38]

{62} Montaigne page 252[39]

There are some Persons... who have believed that the many difficulties which attend our little Degree of Knowledge, the great Number of Systems, the various Emblems of Human

---

[37] John Milton, *Paradise Lost*, Book IV. (1667)

[38] Joseph Addison, writing in *The Spectator*, Wednesday, 14 March 1711.

[39] Lord C mis-attributes this passage to Montaigne. In fact it is from Francesco Algarotti's *Sir Isaac Newton's Philosophy Explain'd For the Use of the Ladies*, vol. 2, The Sixth Dialogue (London: 1739). Algarotti (1712-1764) was a Venetian born polymath, a friend of Frederick the Great, and with several contacts in England.

Ignorance, and that continual tantalizing which philosophers suffer in their Searches after Truth, proceed from no other Cause than our want of a Sixth Natural Sense which might reveal a great Part of what is at present hid from us, and escapes perhaps those five Senses given us by Nature [to lay hold on external Objects, and bring them to the Mind].

As there are certain Animals among us, who, by virtue of Senses, of which we perhaps have no Knowledge, foresee the change of the Seasons, and approach of the Morning, and, without having read **{63}** Dioscorides[40] or any other Botanist, can amidst a thousand others distinguish that salutary Herb that cures their Hurts, who knows but in some other System,[(in the World of *Jupiter* perhaps[41],)] there may be Animals which, more sharpsighted than our philosophers, may discover the size of those

---

[40] Pedanius Dioscorides (ca.40-90 ad) a Greek botanist, whose *De materia medica* was still being consulted into the 19th century.

[41] Jupiter is the largest planet in our solar system, known since ancient times. The Romans named it after the king of their gods. Saturn is the slowest of the planets (and the furthest from us) named after the god of Time (& agriculture). The rings of Saturn were first seen by Galileo, and were later identified as particles..

particles that compose the variety of Colours, and in what manner, without the assistance of Ropes or Pullies, they may attract Saturn at a Distance of more than 350 Millions of Miles?

{64} The Moderation of Sir I. Newton, in never affirming any Thing to be true which was not demonstrated by Observation, may serve for an example to the most rash Asserters. Who could have more reason to think himself capable of ascending Heaven, or bringing the Secrets of Nature in Triumph from thence, than He, who, poised upon the Wings of Geometry, could take his Flight through Immense Spaces, till then impenetrable to human Curiosity?[42]

{66}[43] Dr Morgan: Theology page 301[44]
Man, by the general Law and Constitution of Nature, is placed at the Head of this inferior Part of the Creation, and made Lord over all the

---

[42] This paragraph occurs slightly earlier in the Sixth Dialogue with the Marchioness.
[43] p. 65 is blank
[44] Thomas Morgan, *Physico-theology: or, a philosophico-moral disquisition concerning human nature, free agency, moral government, and divine providence*, Ch. VII, pp. 301-303, 318 & pp. 319-20. (1741). Dr Morgan (1672-1743) was a former Presbyterian minister turned physician and Christian deist.

Works of God below; his natural Dominion extends from the Lion to the Fly, and to the minutest Insect within his Notice; he prescribes the Laws and Conditions of Life to them, and is made Arbiter and Judge how far, and in what Cases they are to be preserved and cherished, or destroyed and rooted out.

These Creatures know nothing of the Knowledge, Art, and Contrivances of Man, of his Capacity, Powers and Ways of acting, or by what Means they are often destroyed by Thousands in a Moment.

{67} Suppose now any Species of those small Insects, that know no more of us, than we do of any superior, invisible Beings above us; suppose them, I say, to be endued with Reason, such as ours, their original Senses, and Means of taking in the Notice of Things from without, remaining the same as before: What would they think, or how must they reason about an infinite Number of Incidents and Accidents that befall them by the Art and Contrivance of Man, and of which they can assign no Cause? Some of then, perhaps, would resolve their Fate into Chance, and imagine there could be no Reason, Wisdom, Design, or Contrivance in what had happened. Others would conclude, it must be the immediate **{68}** Hand and Power of God, or something which he had done by a particular miraculous Interposition, contrary to the general established Laws of Nature. But we are sure that both these reasoning Insects would be wrong, because they nothing of Man, or of his Powers and Ways of acting above them. These would be the vulgar Insects, and such their Reasoning: But, perhaps, there might be some among them of a more philosophical Genius, who had carried their Researches and Views of Nature a little farther; and these would conclude, from a Parity of Reason, and **{69}** Analogy of Nature, that as there are an Infinity of Creatures below them, many of which had been subjected to them, and by the Law of Nature put into their Power, so there must be superior Ranks and Orders of Beings above them, of whose Powers, Capacities, and Ways of acting, they could not judge, and yet, that these superior Beings, tho' invisible or unknown to them, might have Power to do them good or hurt, to save or destroy them, in Consequence of the Law of their Nature, and to answer the Ends of Providence, or divine Government.

We know that such Reasonings and Conclusions would be right in Bees, Ants, etc **{70}** were they endued with that Faculty; and we have the same Reason and Analogy of Nature, thar there are still Beings above us, as much superior to us in all Degrees of Perfection, as we are to the meanest Fly or Insect. There can be no Reason to doubt, but such superior Intelligences, as free Agents, have Power **to** act upon the Elements, and direct natural Causes, by Ways and Means unknown to us. The Art of Man, by applying Actives to Passives, in a Way of natural Mechanism, can produce the most surprising Phenomena.....

{71} ... And since Man, by Reasoning and Discourse, or by suggesting a Thought, have such a Power and Influence over one another, without destroying Liberty or free Agency, since this, I say, may be done in a visible and sensible Way, who can doubt but superior intelligent Beings, and free Agents, may have te same Power and Influence over us, as we have over one another, or the inferior Creatures? And why may not this be as much a general Constitution and Law of Nature, as what we observe, visibly and sensibly, with respect to our own Powers and Faculties?... (pp. 301-3)

.... A single Thought suggested or incidentally thrown in upon the mind, shall alter at once a Man's scheme of action, and set him upon a new projection.... (p. 318)

{72} ...But still, all such superior Influence and Direction must be agreeable to the Law of

Nature in the Creature, which is to be thus influenced and governed. We can impress the Senses, Appetites ad Passions of the inferior brute Creatures, but cannot inform their Understanding and Reason; we cannot give them the Notions and Ideas of general, abstract Truth, or direct and govern them in that Way: We must act upon them by such Means as are suitable to the Natures and Capacities. No Body should pretend to make a Parrot a Logician, or Ape an Astronomer. And in like Manner, whatever Power or Influence superior Beings may have over us, they must apply to our Understanding and Reason, such as it is, and could not inform or govern us by any Light above Reason. They could not... (pp. 319-20)

The text here ends abruptly, in mid-sentence. It seems likely that the first notebook was rebound (the pages are trimmed) and that, when the next notebook was bound in, the end of the first notebook was lost.

THE SECOND NOTEBOOK

{1}

Modest Doubt is call'd
The Beacon of the Wise, the Tent that searches
To the bottom of the worst[45]

...Reason flies the Object of all Harm[46]

We may not think the justness of each act
Such and no other than event doth form it, [47]

The amity that wisdom knits not,
Folly may easily untie.[48]

Pride is [his own glass], his own Trumpet, his
own
Chronicle, and whatever praises itself
but in the Deed, devours te Deed in
the praise[49].

---

[45] Hector to Priam, Shakespeare, *Troilus & Cressida*, Act II, Scene II.
[46] Troilus to Helenus, Shakespeare, *Troilus & Cressida*, Act II, Scene II
[47] Troilus to Hector, Shakespeare, *Troilus & Cressida*, Act II, Scene II
[48] Ulysses in Shakespeare, *Troilus & Cressida*, Act II, Scene III
[49] Agamemnon to Ajax, Shakespeare, *Troilus &*

Those wounds heal ill that Men do give themselves.[50]

{2} [Troilus:] Fears make devils of Cherubins; they never see truly.
[Cressida:] Blind fear, that seeing reason leads, finds safer footing than blind reason, stumbling without fear. To fear the worst oft cures the worse.[51]

Our very eyes are sometimes, like our judgements, blind.[52]

Wisely and slow, they stumble that run fast.[53]

Fear does half the work of Lying Fame,
And Cowards thus their own Misfortunes Frame:
By their own feigning Fancies are betray'd,
And groan beneath those Ills themselves have made. [54]

Cressida, Act II, Scene III
[50] Patroclus to Achilles, Shakespeare, *Troilus & Cressida*, Act III, Scene III
[51] *Troilus & Cressida*, Act III, Scene II
[52] Imogen in Shakespeare, *Cymbeline*, Act IV, Scene II.
[53] Friar Laurence to Romeo, Shakespeare, *Romeo & Juliet*, Act II, Scene III.

Car'd to page 53[55]

{3} …No Man is the lord of anything [-
Though in and of him there be much consisting -
]
Till he communicate his parts to others;
Nor doth he of himself know them for
ought, till he behold them formed
in th' applause where they're extended;
which like an arch reverberates the
voice again[56]

Perseverance[, dear my lord,] keeps Honour
Bright.
To have done is to hang quite out
of fashion like a rusty mail in
monumental mockery[57]

All with one consent praise new born
Gauds, tho' they are made of things past…..
The present Eye praises the present Object[58]

---

[54]Lucan, *The Civil War*, Book I, 485-6, translated by Henry Baker, *Medulla Poetarum Romanorum*, Vol. Ii, (1737)
[55] Further poems on the theme of fear come later in Lord C's book.
[56] Ulysses to Achilles, Shakespeare, *Troilus & Cressida*, Act III, Scene III, 120-126
[57] Ulysses to Achilles, Shakespeare, *Troilus & Cressida*, Act III, Scene III, 155-158

{4} Give thy thoughts no Tongue,
Nor any unproportioned thought his Act.
Be thou familiar, but by no means Vulgar.
Those friends thou hast, and their Adoption tried,
Grapple them to thy Soul with hoops of Steel;
But do not dull thy palm with entertainment
Of each new-hatch'd, unfledged Comrade...

... Give every man thy ear, but few thy voice;
Take each man's Censure, but reserve thy Judgment...

...This above all: to thine own self be true,
And it must follow, as the Night the Day,
Thou canst not then be false to any Man...[59]

{5} Jealousy
It seems it is as proper to our age
To cast beyond ourselves in our opinions
As it is common for the younger sort
To lack discretion.[60]

---

[58] Ulysses to Achilles, Shakespeare, *Troilus & Cressida*, Act III, Scene III, 176-177, 180-181
[59] Polonius to Laertes, Shakespeare, *Hamlet*, Act I, Scene III, 59-64, 68-69, 78-80
[60] Polonius to Ophelia, Shakespeare, *Hamlet*, Act II, Scene I, 114-117

The great Man down, you mark his favourite flies.
The poor advanced makes friends of Enemies.
And hitherto doth love on fortune tend,
For who not needs shall never lack a Friend,
And who in want a hollow friend doth try,
Directly seasons him his Enemy.[61]

Virtue itself of vice must pardon beg,
Yea, curb and woo, for leave to do him good.[62]

{6} Custom

That monster, custom, who all sense doth eat,
Of habits devil, is angel yet in this:
That to the use of actions fair and good
He likewise gives a frock or livery
That aptly is put on...
... For use almost can change the stamp of nature,
And either rein the devil or throw him out
With wondrous potency. [63]

Habit to page 22[64]

---

[61] The Player King, Shakespeare, *Hamlet*, Act III, Scene II, 199-204

[62] Hamlet to the Queen, Shakespeare, *Hamlet*, Act III, Scene IV, 154-155

[63] Hamlet to the Queen, Shakespeare, *Hamlet*, Act III, Scene IV, 163-167, 170-172

[64] In that excerpt, Hamlet is referring to the King's drunkenness, so Lord C. is here referring to a later section in his notebook on the 'Habit' of sobriety.

{7} What is a Man,
If his chief good and Marker of his time
Be but to sleep and feed? a Beast, no more.
Sure, he that made us with such large discourse,
Looking before and after, gave us not
That capability and god-like reason
To rust in us unused. [65]

How poor are they that have no patience!
What wound did ever heal but by degrees?[66]

'tis meet
That noble minds keep ever with their likes;
For who so firm that cannot be seduced?[67]

{8} Gold
Why, this [ye Gods] will lug your priests
and Servants from your
sides, pluck stout men's pillows
from below their heads:
This yellow slave
Will knit and break religions,
bless the accursed, Make the hoar

---

[65] Hamlet's soliloquy, Shakespeare, *Hamlet*, Act IV, Scene IV, 36-42
[66] Iago in Shakespeare, *Othello*, Act II, Scene III, 358-359
[67] Cassius' soliloquy, in Shakespeare, *Julius Caesar,* Act I, Scene II, 309-311

leprosy adored, place thieves
and give them title, knee and approbation
with senators on the bench:[68]

{9} What can be avoided
Whose end is purposed by the mighty Gods?
... Cowards die many times before their death
The valiant never taste of death but once. [69]

Out, out, brief candle!
Life's but a walking shadow, a poor player
That struts and frets his hour upon the Stage
And then is heard no more: it is a tale
Told by an idiot, full of sound and fury,
Signifying nothing.[70]

{10} ...ever note [Lucilius],

When love begins to sicken and decay,
It useth an enforced ceremony.
There are no tricks in plain and simple faith;[71]

---

[68] Timon's soliloquy, in Shakespeare, *Timon of Athens*, Act IV, Scene III, 30-37

[69] Caesar to Calphurnia, in Shakespeare, *Julius Caesar*, Act II, Scene II, 27, 32-33

[70] Macbeth in Shakespeare, *Macbeth*, Act V, Scene V, 23-28

[71] Brutus to Lucilius, in Shakespeare, *Julius Caesar*, Act IV, Scene II, 19-21

Do what you will, dishonour shall be humour[72]

In time we hate that which we often fear[73]

{11} There is a tide in the affairs of men.
Which, taken at the flood, leads on to fortune;
Omitted, all the voyage of their life
Is bound in shallows and in miseries.[74]

O hateful Error, Melancholy's Child,
Why dost thou show to the apt thoughts of Men
The things that are not? O error, soon conceived,
Thou never comest unto a happy birth
But kill'st the mother that engendered thee![75]

{12} Canst thou not minister to a mind diseased,
Pluck from the memory a rooted sorrow,
Raze out the written troubles of the brain
And with some sweet oblivious antidote

---

[72] Brutus to Cassius, in Shakespeare, *Julius Caesar*, Act IV, Scene III, 108

[73] Charmian to Cleopatra, in Shakespeare, *Antony & Cleopatra*, Act I, Scene 3, 12

[74] Brutus to Cassius, in Shakespeare, *Julius Caesar*, Act IV, Scene III, 216-219

[75] Messala to Titinius, in Shakespeare, *Julius Caesar*, Act V, Scene 3, 67-70

Cleanse the full bosom of that perilous stuff
Which weighs upon the heart?[76]

Cosmus, Duke of Florence, had
a stinging Apothegm against
perfidious [or neglecting] Friends,
[as if those wrongs were unpardonable.]
"You shall read," says he, "that we
are commanded to forgive our
Enemies; but you never read that
we are commanded to forgive our Friends."[77]

{13} To be traduced by Tongues
'Tis but the fate of place, and the rough brake
That virtue must go through. We must not stint
Our necessary actions in the fear
To cope malicious censurers, which ever,
As ravenous fishes, do a vessel follow
That is new trimmed,[78]

Things done well,
And with a care, exempt themselves from fear;[79]

---

[76] Macbeth to Doctor, in Shakespeare, *Macbeth*, Act V, Scene III, 41-44
[77] Francis Bacon, *Essays*, IV, Of Revenge, 74
[78] Wolsey, in Shakespeare, *Henry VIII*, Act 1, Scene II, 75-80
[79] Henry VIII, in Shakespeare, *Henry VIII*, Act 1, Scene II, 88-89

{14} This is the state of man:

To-day he puts forth
The tender leaves of hopes; to-morrow blossoms,
and bears his blushing honours thick upon him;
The third day comes a frost, a killing frost,
[And, when he thinks, good easy man, full surely
His greatness is a-ripening,] nips his root,
And then he falls,[80]

too much honour:
O, 'tis a burthen, [Cromwell, 'tis a burthern]
too heavy for a Man that hopes for heaven, [81]

... The suffrage if the wise,
The praise that's worth ambition, is attained
By sense alone, and dignity of Mind.[82]

{15}
Fling away Ambition:

---

[80] Henry VIII, in Shakespeare, *Henry VIII*, Act III, Scene II, 352-358

[81] Henry VIII, in Shakespeare, *Henry VIII*, Act III, Scene II, 383-385

[82] From *The Art of Preserving Health* (1744), Book IV, The Passions, 279-281, by Dr John Armstrong (1709-1779), an Irish physician, poet & satirist.

By that sin fell the Angels; how can Man, then,
(The Image of his maker) hope to win it?
Love thyself last, [cherish those hearts that hate the;]
Corruption wins not more than honesty.
Still in thy right hand carry gentle peace
To silence envious tongues. Be just, and fear not:
Let all the ends thou aimest at be thy country's
Thy God's, and truth's; then if thou fallest [O, Cromwell]
Thou fall'st a blessed Martyr.[83]

The gawdy gloss of Fortune only strikes
The vulgar Eye[84]

{16} Physiognomy

The Art of knowing the humour, temperament, or disposition of a person, from observations of the lines of the face....

...of all the fanciful Arts of the Ancients, difused among the Moderns, there is none has so much foundation in Nature as this.

---

[83] Henry VIII, in Shakespeare, *Henry VIII*, Act III, Scene II, 440-449

[84] From *The Art of Preserving Health* Book IV, The Passions, 278-279

There is an apparent correspondence between the Face and the Mind; the features and lineaments of the one are directed by the motions and affections of the other: there is even a peculiar arrangement of the members of the Face, a peculiar disposition of the Countenance to each particular affection; perhaps to each particular Idea of the mind.

{17} In effect, the language of the face, *Physiognomy*, is as copious, may, perhaps, as distinct and intelligible as that of the Tongue[, *Speech*,] Thanks to bounteous Nature, she has not confined us to one only Method of conversing with each other, and of learning each other's Thoughts; we have several: We don't wholly depend on the Tongue, which may happen to be bound; and the Ear, which may be deaf; but in those cases we have another recourse, the countenance and the eye; which affords us this further advantage, that, by comparing the reports of the Tongue (a Member exceedingly liable to deceive) with those of the Face, the prevarications of the former may be detected.

{18} The foundation of physiognomy is this: the different objects that present themselves, nay, the different Ideas that arise in the mind, do each make some impression on the spirits; and each impression correspondent or adequate to its cause; therefore each a different impression.

If it be asked how such an impression should be effected; it is easy to answer, that it follows from the Oeconomy of the Creator, who has fix'd such a relation between the several parts of the Creation; to the end we may be apprized of the Approach or Recess of things useful or hurtful to us.... **{19}** The Face here does the office of a Dial-plate; the wheels and springs withinside the machine remaking its muscles, shew what is next to be expected from the striking part...... Now, if by repeated Acts, or the frequent entertaining of a favourite passion, or vice, which natural temperament has hurried, or Custom dragg'd one to, the Face is often put in that position which attends such Acts......[85]and some times unnaturally set in that position.....

This reasoning is confirmed by observation. Thus we see great drinkers, with eyes generally set to the nose, **{20}** the adjacent muscles being oft employed to put them in that position in order to view the loved liquor in the glass at the time of drinking.......

---

[85] From Dr Gwithers' *Discourse of Physiognomy,* 1694

......Hence we may account for the Quakers' expecting face, waiting the [pretended] Spirit[86].

The Melancholy face of most Sectaries, the Studious face of Men of great application of mind etc

Were our observation a little more strict and delicate, we might doubtless not only distinguish Habits and Tempers, but even professions.

{21} In effect, does there need much penetration to distinguish the fierce look of the veteran Soldier, the Contentious look of the practised pleader

The Solemn look of the Ministers of State etc'[87]

---

[86] Lord Catherlough omits Dr Gwithers' 'pretended'. The reputation of the Quakers had changed radically during the previous century.

[87] Dr Gwithers' *Discourse of Physiognomy,* 1694, , but copied (without attribution) by Ephraim Chambers for his popular *Cyclopaedia*, or, *An Universal dictionary of arts and sciences* (1728), which went into several editions and, in its French translation, was the inspiration for Diderot's and d'Alembert's *Encyclopédie*. Lord C. was probably reading Gwithers in Chambers' *Cyclopaedia*, since the extract ends at the point that it ends in Chambers' work.

‘------ the lean gloom that Melancholy wear
The Lover’s paleness; and the sallow hue,
Of Envy, Jealousy; the meagre Stare,
Of Sore Revenge: The cankered Body hence
Betrays each fretful motion of the Mind.’[88]

{22} Habit (from page 6)
In philosophy, an aptitude or disposition either of mind or body, acquiring by a frequent repetition of the same Act.

‘Virtues and Vices are considered by philosophers under the notion of Good and bad Habits.

The Archbishop of Cambray[89] defines Habits, in general, to be certain impressions left in the mind by means whereof we find a greater ease, readiness and inclination to do anything formerly done, by having the Idea ready at hand, to direct us how it was done before -------- Thus we form a habit of sobriety, by having always before us the inconvenience of excess, **{23}** the reflections whereof, being often

---

[88] From *The Art of Preserving Health* (1744) by Dr John Armstrong
[89] François Fénelon (1651-1715) whose best known work *The Adventures of Telemachus* was published in 1699.

repeated, renders the exercise of that virtue more easy.

Fr Malebranche[90] gives a more Mechanical Theory of the Habits ---- his principle is that they consist in a facility which the Spirits have acquired of passing from one part of the Body to another. He argues this: if the mind act on, and move the body, it is, in all probability, by means of a stock of animal spirits lodged in the Brain, ready to be sent at the motion of the will by means of the nerves which open or terminate in the Brain, into the muscles of the Body. **{24}** Now an influx of spirits into a muscle occasions a swelling and of consequence a shortening of the muscle and consequently a motion of the part that muscle is fastened to.

Further, the Spirits do not always find all the Roads open and free, which they are to pass through, whence that difficulty we perceive of moving the fingers with that quickness necessary to play on a musical instrument, or of moving the muscle necessary to pronounce the words of a foreign language.

---

[90] Nicolas Malebranche (1638-1715) a French priest & rationalist philosopher.

{25} But by degrees the spirits, by their continual flux, smoothen the way, so that at length they meet with no resistance at all. Now it is this facility, the spirits find in passing, when directed into the members of the body, that Habit consists.

On this Hypothesis, it is easy accounting for an infinity of phenomenon relating to the Habits ------ why for instance Children acquire new Habits with more ease than grown persons – why it is difficult getting rid of inveterate Habits – whence that incredible quickness in the pronunciation of words, even without thinking of them.

{26} On this footing, the faculty of Memory appears to have very much the Name of a Habit, insomuch that in one sense, it may pass for a Habit.'[91]

{27} Memory
A power or faculty of the mind whereby it retains or recollects the simple Ideas or Images of things before seen imagined understood etc

Of all the Faculties, there is none harder to account for or that has perplexed philosophers

---

[91] From *Cyclopaedia, or an Universal Dictionary of the Arts and Sciences,* by Ephraim Chambers

more than the memory. Some will have it a mere Organ, as the Eye, Ear etc'[92]

{28} is blank

{29} Anger

To pretend utterly to extinguish Anger is but a Stoical Ostentation. We have a better Oracle: be Angry but Sin not: Let not the Sun go down upon your Wrath. Anger must be limited and confined both in point of height and duration.

To allay a Habit or natural inclination to anger, there is no better way, than to reflect seriously upon the calamities and disturbance it occasions in Life. The Scripture exhorts us "To possess our Souls in patience"[93] and certainly whoever is out of patience is out of the possession of his Soul.

{30} To consider it justly Anger is a mean thing, below the Dignity of a Man; as appears by the weakness of those in whom it principally reigns; viz. children, women, the aged and the sick, and therefore if a man happen to be angry, let him, if he would not forget his dignity, carry his anger, not with Tears, but Contempt of the

---

[92] From *Cyclopaedia, or an Universal Dictionary of the Arts and Sciences*

[93] Luke 21:19

person, so as to seem above the injury offered.[94] 'Solomon says, "It is the Glory of a Man to pass over a Transgression"[95]. What is past is irrevocable **{31}** and wise men find it enough, to regard what is present and to come: those therefore do but trifle and disquiet themselves in vain who labour about what is past.

'No man does wrong but to procure himself either profit, pleasure, Honour or the like. Why therefore should I be angry with a Man for loving himself better than me?

'And if a Man should do wrong merely out of ill nature, yet 'tis but like the Thorn, or the Briar, which prick and scratch because it is their Nature.'

{32} Revenge .

'This is certain, he who studies Revenge, and keeps his own wound green, which would otherwise heal.'[96]

{33} Man's power how limited

'Man who is the Servant and Interpreter of Nature, can act and understand no further than

---

[94] Francis Bacon, Lord Verulam, *The Essays or Counsels, Civil or Moral* (1625): Of Anger.
[95] Proverbs 19:11
[96] Francis Bacon, Lord Verulam, *The Essays or Counsels, Civil or Moral*: Of Revenge.

he has either in operation or in contemplation, observed of the method and order of nature.

'Human Knowledge is acquired by Observation and Experience, or by Conversing with the Things about is through the Mediation of the Senses, and subsequent reflexion; therefore the more we observe and try, the more we are enabled to perform, and thus knowledge and power go hand in hand. The Europeans exceed the Savage Indians in power, by having a superior Knowledge of art, arms etc.

{34} Power and Knowledge incide

The Knowledge and power of Man are Coincident: for whilst ignorant of causes, he can produce no effects: nor is Nature to be conquered but by Submission (and that which in speculation stands for the Cause, is what in practice stands for the Rule) viz. by condescending to enquire into an observe her methods of working: as a servant who would learn of his master. For no power of man can possibly break the chain of natural causes; so that the only method whereby men can rule nature, must depend on learning her ways.

{35}

In works, man can do no more than put natural Bodies together, and take them asunder. All the

rest is performed by the internal Operations of Nature.
The Mechanic, the Mathematician, the physician, the Chemist,[and the natural magician][97] are concerned in the works of Nature, but all of them at present superficially, and to little purpose. The knowledge of which Mankind are hitherto possessed does not reach to certainty; and the production of great effects. Physicians pronounce many diseases incurable and frequently fail in the cure of the rest.[98]

{36} Lord Bacon - Aphorisms
[continued from *Novum Organum Scientiarum*]... 'the Alchemist never relinquishes his Hopes: [the works of the natural magician are unstable, and of little advantage][99] the Mechanic Arts derive no great light from philosophy; and but languidly prosecute

---

[97] Lord Catherlough leaves out and 'the natural magician' which is in Bacon's text. In Bacon's day, natural magic included not only astrology and alchemy, but also astronomy and chemistry. There was a gradual separation towards the end of the seventeenth century, though Isaac Newton was committed to alchemical studies.
[98] Francis Bacon, Lord Verulam, *Novum Organum Scientiarum* (1620), Part I, Section I
[99] In Bacon's text, but omitted by Lord Catherlough.

experiments, in low and trivial subjects, so that the discoveries at present in use are extremely Crude and far from perfect.'

'The Root of all the Mischief in the Sciences is this: that falsely magnifying and admiring the powers of the mind, we seek not its real helps. The Subtilty of Nature far exceeds the Subtilty of the Sense and understanding, so that the Sublime {37} Meditations, Speculations and Reasonings of Men, are but a kind of madness.

This aphorism deserves attention certainly upon examining, every man may find, his common notion of Things very inadequate; or far from Corresponding even with those he Gains by conversing more familiarly and intimately with Nature. And yet after a life spent upon any particular enquiry, in the common method, there still usually remains some subtilty of Nature behind, which we cannot catch and are apt perhaps very extravagantly to guess at, **{38}** and if this be the case in sensible and material things, what must our general Theories and Systems be.'

{39} blank

{40} Of Gardens – for the Months December, January etc

A Garden refreshes and recreates the Spirits, insomuch that without it, Buildings and palaces are but gross Handyworks; that have nothing of Nature in them.

For December, January, and the latter part of November choose such things as are green all winter, viz. Holly, Ivy, Bays, Juniper, Cypress, Periwinkle, the white, the purple and the blue, Yews, Box, pines, Firs, Rosemary, Lavender, Germander, the several kinds of Iris, Orange & Lemon trees and Myrtle, if preserved in the Greenhouse, as also sweet Marjoram, set to the warm sun.

{41} For the latter end of January and February there are the Mezereon Tree, which then blossoms; the Crocus Vernus, both the Yellow and the Grey, primroses, anemonies, the early Tuliup, te Oriental Hyacinth, the Chamairis, and the Fritillaria.

For March, there are Violets of all kids, especially the single Blue which are the earliest; the Yellow Daffadil, the Daisy, the Almond Tree, the Cornel Tree in blossom, and the Sweet-Briar.

In April, follow the double white violets, the Wall flower, the Stock-Gilliflower, the Cowslip, the Flower-de-Luce, Lillies of all kinds, Rosemary Flowers; the Tulip, the double piony, the pale Daffadil, the French Honeysuckle, **{42}** the Cherry Tree, the pear, and all the plumb trees in Blossom; the Bearsbreech in leaf, and the Lelach tree.

In May and June come pinks of all sorts, especially the blush pink; Roses of all kinds; except the Musk-Rose which comes later, Honeysuckles, Strawberries, Bugloss, Columbine, the french Marygold; Flos Africanus, single and double, the Cherry tree in fruit, Currants, Figs in fruit, the vine in flower, Lavender in flower, **{43}** the Garden Satyrion with the white flower, Herba Muscaria, the Lilly of the Valley, and the Apple tree in blossom.

In July come Gilliflowers of all sorts, Musk Roses, the lime tree in Blossom, early peas, plumbs and apples in fruit.

in August, come plumbs of all sorts in fruit, pears, apricots, Barberries, Filberds, Muskmelons, and Monkshoods of all colours.

in September come Grapes, Apples, poppies if all colours, peaches, Melocotones, Nectarines, Cornels, Wardens, Quinces.

{44} In October and the beginning of November come Services, Medlars, Sloes, Roses cut or removed to come later, Holly-oaks etc. The plants here mentioned are for the Climate of London, but our meaning is to show, how a kind of perpetual spring may be procured in other places also, according to their Nature.

And because the Odour of Flowers is much sweeter in the air (where it undulates, like the warbling of Musick) than when in the Hand, nothing contributes more to procure the pleasure of their free scent, than to know what plants best perfume the air, while growing.

Roses, both the Damask and the Red, are, whilst on the Bush,**{45}** retentive of their Odour; or perfume the Air so little that you mat walk by a whole Hedge-Row of them, without perceiving their Sweetness, even on a dewy morning. Bays, Rosemary, and sweet marjoram likewise yield little scent as they grow.

What most perfumes the Air whilst growing is the violet, especially the white double violet, which flowers twice a year, viz about the middle of April and towards the end of August. Next to this is the Musk-Rose; then comes the Strawberry leaves, which as they wither yield an excellent Cordial Odour: then the vine blossoms, which appear **{46}** like Dust upon the

Stalk of a Bent; the next in order is the sweet Briar, then wall flowers, which are very delightful if set under a parlour window: then pinks and Gilliflowers; then the flowers of the Lime Tree; then the Honeysuckle at some small distance: ad lastly the Flowers of Lavender. We do not mention Bean-blossoms, because they are Field flowers.

The plants which agreeably perfume the air, not when growing but by being trampled upon and crushed, are three viz. Burnet, Wild Thyme and Water Mint. Therefore whole walks should be **{47}** planted with them; so have the pleasure of their Odour in walking upon them.'[100]

{48} Melancholy
Tis the great art of life to manage well the restless mind....

... Chiefly where solitude, sad nurse of Care
To sickly musing gives the pensive mind;
There madness enters, and the dim-ey'd Fiend,

---

[100] Francis Bacon, Lord Verulam, *The Essays or Counsels, Civil or Moral* (1625): Of Gardens. It contains some of the most famous lines in garden history and is still the most read of his works. Though it reads as quite a humble *vade mecum* of gardening, Bacon intended it as a guide to the garden of a great house or palace.

Sour Melancholy, night and day provokes
Her own eternal wound. The sun grows pale
A mournful visionary light overspreads
The cheerful face of Nature; earth becomes
A weary desert, and heaven frowns above
Then various shapes of cursed illusion [rise
Whate'er the wretched fears,] creative fear
Forms out of nothing **{49}** and with monsters teems,
Unknown in hell. The prostrate soul beneath
A load of huge imagination heaves
And all the horrors that the guilty feels
With anxious flutterings wake the Guiltless breast.....

...Oft from the body, by long ails mistuned,
This evil springs, the most important health,
That of the mind, destroy; and when the mind
They first invade, the conscious body soon
In sympathetic languishment declines......

... Add that your means, your health, your parts decay
{50} Your friends avoid you, brutishly transform'd
They hardly know you, or if one remains
To wish you well, he wishes you in heaven.
Despis'd, unwept, you fall, who might have left

A sacred, cherish'd, sadly pleasing name
A name still to be uttered with a sigh
Your last ungraceful scene has quite effac'd
'All sense and memory of your former worth.....

{51} ... Those chronic passions, while from real woes
They rise, and yet without the bodies fault
Infest the soul, admit one only cure;
Diversion, hurry, and a restless life.
Vain are the consolations of the wise,
In vain your friends would reason down your pain....

...Go, seek the cheerful haunts
Of men, and mingle with the bustling crowd;
Lay schemes of wealth, or power, or fame, the wish
Of nobler minds, and push them night and day....

{52} I would invoke new Passions to your aid:
With indignation would extinguish Fear,
With Fear or generous Pity vanquish Rage,
And Love with Pride; and force to force oppose.'[101]

---

[101] From *The Art of Preserving Health* (1744) by Dr John Armstrong (1709-1779), a Scottish physician (practising in London) and a poet, part of a literary scene that included James Thomson.

'Then let us not of Fate complain
For soon shall change the gloomy scene….
When Fortune, various goddess, lowers,
Collect your strength, exert your powers:
But when she breathes as kinder gale,
Be wise, and furl your swelling sail.'[102]

{53} from page 2 - Fear

Ah! From your bosoms banish, if you can,
Those fatal guests: and first the Daemon Fear;
That trembles at impossible events,
Lest aged Atlas should resign his load,
And heav'n's eternal battlements rush down,
Is there an evil worse than fear itself?
And what avails it that indulgent heaven
From mortal eyes has wrapt the woes to come,
If we, ingenious to torment ourselves,
Grow pale at hideous fictions of our own?
Enjoy the present; nor with heedless cates,
{54} Of what may spring from blind
Misfortune['s womb],
Appal the surest hour that life bestows.
Serene, and master of yourself, prepare
For what may come; and leave the rest to
heaven.'

---

[102] Horace, Ode X. *To Lucinius Murena,*

{55} By its own toil the gross corporeal frame
Fatigues, extenuates, or destroys itself.
Nor less the labours of the mind corrode
The solid fabric: for by subtle parts
And viewless atoms, secret nature moves
The mighty wheels of this stupendous world.
By subtle fluids pour'd through subtle tubes
The natural vital functions are perform'd,
By these the stubborn aliments are tamed;
The toiling heart distributes life and strength....

[... 'Tis painful Thinking that corrodes our clay....

...There is, they say (and believe there is)
A spark within us of the immortal sire,
That animates and moulds the crosser frame,
And when the body sinks escapes to heav'n,
Its native seat, and mixes with the gods:
Meanwhile this heav'nly particle pervades
The mortal elements, in every nerve
It trills with pleasure, or grows mad with pain
And, in the secret conclave, as it feels
The body's woes and joys, this ruling power
Wields at its will the dull material world,
And is the body's Health or malady....][103]

---

[103] This page – following on from p. 55 – interrupts the poem, which continues from the end of p.55 to

{56} ...These the still-crumbling frame rebuild; and these
Are lost in thinking, and dissolve in air.

But 'tis not Thought (for still the Soul's employed)
'Tis painful thinking that corrodes our Clay
All day the vacant eye without fatigue
Strays o'er the heaven and earth; but long intent
On microscopic arts its vigour fails.
Just so the mind, with various thought amused,
Nor aches itself, nor gives the Body pain.
{57} But anxious study, discontent, and Care,
Love without hope, and Hate without revenge,
And Fear, and Jealousy, fatigue the Soul,
Engross the subtle ministers of life,
And spoil the lab'ring functions of their share.
Hence the lean gloom that melancholy wears;
The lover's paleness; and the sallow hue
Of Envy, Jealousy; the meagre stare
Of sore Revenge: the canker'd body hence
Betrays each fretful motion of the mind.

---

the beginning of p. 56. It is given a number – 5.. – which is no longer legible.

{58} **Virtue**, the strength and beauty of the soul,
Is the best Gift of heaven: a happiness
That even above the smiles and frowns of fate
Exalts great Nature's favourites...

...'Tis not for mortals always to be blest.
But him the least the dull or painful hours
Of life oppress, whom sober sense conducts,
And Virtue, thro' this labyrinth we tread.
Virtue and Sense I mean not to disjoin;
Virtue and Sense are one: and, trust me, he
who has not virtue is not truly wise..

{59} Virtue... is sometimes angry, and its frown confounds;
'Tis even vindictive, but in vengeance just.
Knaves fain would laugh at it; some great ones dare;
But at his heart the most undaunted son
Of fortune dreads its name and awful Charms.
To noblest uses this determines wealth;
This is the solid pomp of prosperous days;
The peace and shelter of adversity....
.....The gawdy gloss of Fortune only strikes
The vulgar eye: the suffrage of the wise,
{60} The praise that's worth ambition, is attained
By Sense alone, and dignity of mind.

Happiness

Our aim is happiness....
'tis the pursuit of all that live;
Yet few attain it, if 'twas e'er attain'd.
But they the widest wander from the mark,
Who thro' the flow'ry paths of saunt'ring Joy
Seek this coy Goddess; that from stage to stage
Invites us still, but shifts as we pursue.
For, not to name the pains that pleasure brings
To counterpoise itself, relentless fate
{61} Forbids that we thro' gay voluptuous wilds,
Should ever roam: and were the Fates more
kind,
Our narrow luxuries would soon grow stale.
Were these exhaustless, Nature would grow
sick,
And, cloyed with pleasure, squeamishly
complain
That all is vanity, and life a dream.
Let nature rest: be busy for yourself,
And for your friend; be busy even in vain
Rather than teize her sated appetites.
{62} Who never fasts, no banquet e'er enjoys;
Who never toils or watches, never sleeps.
Let nature rest: and when the taste of joy
Grows keen, indulge; but shun satiety.

Hope

Whatever chearful and serene
Supports the mind, supports the Body too.
Hence, the most vital movement mortals feel
Is Hope; the balm and life--blood of the soul.
It pleases, and it lasts. Indulgent Heaven
Sent down the kind delusion, thro' the paths
{63} Of rugged life to lead us patient on;
And make our happiest state no tedious thing.
Our greatest good, and what we least can spare,
Is Hope: the last of all our evils, Fear. [104]

Love, Hope, and Joy, fair pleasure's smiling train,
Hate, Fear, and Grief, the Family of pain,
These mixed with art, and to due bounds confined,
Make and maintain the Balance of the mind;
M. Pope[105]

{64} Passions

"The ruling passion, be it what it will,
The ruling passion conquers reason still."
Pope[106]

---

[104] From *The Art of Preserving Health,* Book IV (1744) by Dr John Armstrong

[105] Alexander Pope, *Essay on Man*, Epistle II:III

[106]Alexander Pope, Moral Essays, Epistle I, to Sir

A mightier power the strong direction sends,
And several Men impells to several Ends:
Like varying Winds, by other passions tost,
This drives them constant to a certain coast...
....As fruits, ungrateful to the planter's care,
On savage stocks inserted, learn to bear;
The surest virtues thus from passions shoot,
Wild nature's vigour working at the root.
{65} What Crops of Wit and Honesty appear
From Spleen, from Obstinacy, hate, or Fear!
See Anger, Zeal and Fortitude supply;
Even Avarice, prudence; Sloth, philosophy;[107]
... Envy, to which th' ignoble mind's a slave,
Is emulation in the learned or brave;
Nor virtue, male or female, can we name,
But what will grow on pride, or grow on shame.[108]

{66} We find various Modifications and impressions of pleasure and pain inseparably annexed, by an established Law of Nature, to the several judgements we form concerning Good and Evil.....

Richard Temple, Lord Cobham
[107] Lord C omits 'Lust, through some certain strainers well refined, Is gentle love, and charms all womankind;'
[108] Alexander Pope, *Essay on Man*, Epistle II:III

.....All the passions may be reduced to Love and Hatred, of which Joy and Sorrow, Hope and Fear, are only so many modifications, or complexions, according to the various appearances, positions etc of the Object.[109]

{67-69 are blank}

{70} Exercise - Armstrong

Toil and be strong. By toil the flaccid nerves
Grow firm, and gain a more compacted tone;
The greener juices are by toil subdued.
Mellowed and subtilized; the vapid old
Expelled, and all the rancour of the blood.
Come, my companions, ye who feel the charms
Of nature and the year; come, let us stray
Where chance or fancy leads our roving walk:
Come, while the soft voluptuous breezes fan
The fleecy heavens, inwrap the limbs un balm,
And shed a charming languor o'er the soul.....

{71} Exercise

... if through genuine tenderness of heart,
Or secret want of relish for the game,

[109] From *Cyclopaedia, or an Universal Dictionary of the Arts and Sciences,* by Ephraim Chambers, 'Passion', which is taken from *An Essay on Health and Long Life* (1724), a best-selling self-help manual, by the Scottish physician, George Cheyne (1671-1743).

You shun the glories of the chase,
Nor care to haunt the peopled stream; the garden yields
A soft amusement, a humane delight.
To raise th' insipid nature of the ground
Or tame its savage genius to the grace
Of careless sweet rusticity, that seems
The amiable result of happy chance
Is to create; and gives a godlike joy,
Which every year improves...
..O happy he! Whom, when his years decline

{72} Retirement
(His fortune and his fame by worthy means
Attain'd, and equal to his moderate mind;
His life approved by all the wise and good,
Even envied by the vain) the peaceful groves
Of Epicurus, from this stormy world,
Receive to rest; of all ungrateful cares
Absolved, and sacred from the selfish crowd.
Happiest of men! If the same soil invites
A chosen few, companions of his youth,
Once fellow rakes perhaps, now rural Friends;
With whom in easy commerce to pursue
Nature's free charms, and vie for silvan fame:
{73} A fair ambition; void of strife or guile,
Or jealousy or pain to be outdone....
...Thrice happy days! In rural business pass'd.[110]

{74-76 are blank}

{77} §13 These [three] Laws the Rules of Moral Good and Evil

[These three then,]

1st the Law of God;

2nd the Law of publick Societies;

3rd the Law of Fashion, or private Censure,

are those to which Men variously compare their Actions: and it is by their Conformity to one of these Laws that they take their Measures, when they would judge of their Moral Rectitude, and denominate their actions Good or Bad....

{78} §12 [Its enforcement is commendation and discredit]

... He who imagines Commendation and disgrace not to be strong motives to Men to accommodate themselves to the Opinions and Rules of those with whom they converse, seems little skilled in the Nature or History of Mankind: The greatest part whereof we shall find to govern themselves chiefly, if not solely, by this Law of Fashion; and so they do that which keeps them in Reputation with their Company, little regard the Laws of God, or the Magistrate.

---

[110] pp. 70-73 all from *The Art of Preserving Health,* Book III, by Dr John Armstrong

The penalties that attend the Breach of God's Laws some, nay perhaps most Men, seldom seriously reflect on: and amongst those that do, **{79}** many, whilst they break the law, entertain Thoughts of future Reconciliation, and making their peace for such Breaches.

And as to the punishments due from the Laws of the Commonwealth, they frequently flatter themselves with the hopes of Impunity.

But no man escapes the punishment of their Censure and dislike, who offends against the Fashion and Opinion of the Company he keeps, and would recommend himself to.

Nor is there one of Ten thousand, who is stiff and insensible enough, to bear up **{80}** under the constant dislike and Condemnation of his own [club.

He must be of a strange and unusual constitution, who can content himself to live in the constant disgrace and disrepute with his own][111] particular society.

Solitude many men have sought, and been reconciled to: But nobody that has the least Thought or Sense [of a man about him,] can live in society under the constant dislike and ill

[111] Lord C omits this passage, either by mistake or intentionally.

opinion of his familiars, and those he converses with.
This is a Burthen too heavy for Human Sufferance: and He must be made up of irreconcilable contradictions, who can take pleasure in Company, and yet be insensible of Contempt and Disgrace from his Companions.[112]

{81-87 are blank}

Here it would appear that Lord C started another notebook that was later bound in with first

[112] John Locke, *An Essay concerning Human Understanding*, Ch. XXVIII, Of Other Relations,

THE THIRD NOTEBOOK

{1} Ecclesiasticus, Chap 1st
[v. 12] The fear of the Lord maketh a merry heart, and giveth Joy, and Gladness, and a long Life.

[v. 18] The fear of the Lord is a Crown of Wisdom, making peace and perfect health to flourish; both which are the Gifts of God.

[v.19] Wisdom raineth down Skill and Knowledge of understanding, and exalteth them to Honour that hold her fast.

[v. 20] The root of wisdom is to fear the Lord, and the Branches thereof are long Life. [v. 21 The fear of the Lord driveth away sins:] and where it is present, it turneth away wrath.

[v. 22] A Furious Man cannot be justified; for the sway of his Fury shall be his destruction. [v. 23] A patient Man will bear for a time,[and afterward joy shall spring up unto him. v. 24 He will hide his words for a time,] and the lips of many shall declare his Wisdom.

{2} Chap. 1st and 2nd All Wisdom is from God[113]

---

[113] These headings at the top of the page appear to be Lord C's own composition.

[1: 26] If thou desire wisdom, keep the commandments, and the Lord shall give her unto thee.

[1: 29] Be not an hypocrite in the sight of Men, and take good heed what thou speakest.

[2: 4] Whatsoever is brought upon thee take cheerfully, and be patient when thou art changed to a low estate.

[2: 5] For gold is tried in the fire, and acceptable men in the furnace of adversity.

[2: 6] Believe in him, and he will help thee; order thy way aright, and trust in him.

[2: 10] Look at the generations of old, and see; did ever any trust in the Lord, and was confounded? Or did any abide in his Fear, and was forsaken? or whom did he ever despise, that called upon him?

[2: 11] For the Lord is full of compassion and mercy,[longsuffering, and very pitiful, and forgiveth sins,] and saveth in time of affliction.

{3} Be patient & trust in God, 2nd and 3rd Chap.

[2:12] Woe be to fearful hearts, and faint hands, [and the sinner that goeth two ways! v. 13 Woe unto him that is fainthearted!] for he believeth not; therefore shall he not be defended.

[2:14] Woe unto you that have lost patience: And what will you do, when the Lord shall visit you.

[2: 17-18] They that fear the Lord will prepare their Hearts, and humble their Souls in his sight. Saying we will fall into the hands of the Lord, and not into the hands of Men: For as his Majesty is, so is his mercy.

[3:18] The greater thou art, the more humble Thyself, and Thou shalt find favour before the Lord.

{4} Chap 3rd Christians must help their parents.
[3:10] Glory not in the dishonour of thy Father, For thy Father's dishonour is no Glory unto Thee.

[3:12-13] [My son] Help thy Father in his Age, and grieve him not as long as thou livest. And if his understanding fail, have patience with him; and despise him not when thou art in thy full strength.

[3:15] In the day of thine affliction it shall be remembered; Thy sins also shall melt away, as the Ice in the fair warm weather.

[3:17] My son, go on with thy business in meekness; so shalt thou be beloved of him that is approved.

{5} We may not desire to know all Things
[3:21-25} Seek not out things that are too hard for thee, neither search the things that are above thy strength.

But what is commanded thee, think thereupon with reverence, for it is not needful for thee to see with thine eyes the things that are in secret.

Be not curious in unnecessary matters: for more things are shewed unto thee than men understand.

For many are deceived by their own vain opinion; and an evil suspicion hath overthrown their judgment.

[Without eyes thou shalt want light:] profess not the knowledge [therefore] that thou hast not.

{6} Chap 4 We may not despise the poor.
[4:1-3] [My son,] Defraud not the poor .of his living, and make not the needy eyes to wait long.

Make not an hungry soul sorrowful; neither provoke a man in his distress.

Add not more trouble to an heart that is vexed; and defer not to give to him that is in need.

[4:5-6] [Turn not away thine eye from the needy,] and give him none occasion to curse thee.

For if he curse thee in the bitterness of his soul, his prayer shall be heard of him that made him.

[4:9] Deliver him that suffereth wrong from the hand of his oppressors, and be not fainthearted when thou sittest in judgement.

{7] Seek for Wisdom

[4:15] Whoso giveth ear unto [[wisdom]], shall [judge the nations: and he that attendeth unto her] shall dwell securely.

[4:17-19] [For] At first she will walk with him, by crooked ways, and bring fear and dread upon him, and torment him with her discipline, until she may trust his Soul, and try him by her Laws.

Then will she return the straight way unto him, and comfort him, and show him her secrets.

But if he go wrong, she will forsake him, and give him over to his own ruin.

{8} Chap 4 Not to gainsay the truth

[4:22-25 & 27] Accept no person against thy Soul, and let not the reverence of any Man cause thee to fall.

And refrain not to speak, when there is occasion to do good, and hide not thy wisdom in her beauty.

For by Speech wisdom shall be known: and Learning by the word of the Tongue.

In no wise speak against the Truth; but be abashed of the error of thine ignorance.

[Be not ashamed to confess thy sins; and force not the course of the river.]

Make not thyself an underling to a foolish man; neither accept the person of the mighty.

{9} Not to be as lions in our houses
[4:28-31] Strive for the Truth unto death, and the Lord shall fight for thee.

Be not hasty in thy Tongue, and in thy deeds slack and remiss.

Be not as a Lion in thy house, nor frantic among thy servants.

Let not thine hand be stretched out to receive, and shut when thou shouldest repay.

{10} Chap 5th We must not presume upon our wealth and strength
[5:1-6] Set not thy heart upon thy Goods; and say not, I have enough for my life.

Follow not thine own mind and thy strength, to walk in the ways of thy heart:

and say not, Who shall control me for my works? for the Lord will surely revenge thy pride.

Say not, I have sinned, and what harm hath happened unto me? for the Lord is longsuffering, he will in no wise let thee go.

Concerning propitiation, be not without fear to add Sin unto Sin:

and say not, his Mercy is great; He will be pacified for the multitude of my Sins: for mercy and wrath come from him, and his indignation resteth upon sinners.

{11} ..nor of the Mercy of God to Sin
{5:7] Make no tarrying to turn to the Lord, and put not off from day to day: for suddenly shall the wrath of the Lord come forth, and in thy security thou shalt be destroyed, and perish in the day of vengeance.

[5:8] Set not thine heart upon goods unjustly gotten; for they shall not profit thee in the day of calamity.

[5:15] Be not ignorant of any thing in a great matter or a small.

{12} Chap 5 We must not be double Tongued
[5:10-14] Be steadfast in thy understanding; and let thy word be the same.

Be swift to hear; and let thy life be sincere; and with patience give answer.

If thou hast understanding, answer thy neighbour; if not, lay thy hand upon thy mouth.

Honour and shame is in talk: and the Tongue of Man is his fall.

Be not called a Whisperer, and lie not in wait with thy Tongue: for a foul shame is upon the Thief, and an evil condemnation upon the double Tongue.

{13} Do not extol thine own Council Chap 6th
[6:1-4] Instead of a Friend become not an Enemy; for thereby thou shalt inherit an ill name, shame, and reproach: [even so shall a sinner that hath a double tongue.]

Extol not thyself in the counsel of thine own heart; that thy Soul be not torn in pieces as a Bull straying alone.

Thou shalt eat up thy leaves, and lose thy Fruit, and leave thyself as a dry Tree.

A wicked Soul shall destroy him that hath it, and shall make him to be laughed to scorn of his Enemies.

{14} Chap 6 Make choice of a Friend
[6:5-15] Sweet language will multiply friends: and a fair speaking tongue will increase kind greetings.

Be in peace with many: nevertheless have but one Counsellor of a thousand.

If thou wouldest get a friend, prove him first, and be not hasty to credit him.

For some Man is a friend for his own occasion, and will not abide in the day of thy trouble.

And there is a friend, who being turned to Enmity and strife will discover thy reproach.

Again, some friend is a Companion at the table, and will not continue in the day...

{15}
...of thy affliction.

But in thy prosperity, he will be as thyself, and will be bold over thy servants.

If thou be brought low, he will be against thee, and will hide himself from thy face.

Separate thyself from thine Enemies, and take heed of thy Friends.

A faithful Friend is a strong defence: and he that hath found such an one hath found a Treasure.

Nothing doth countervail a faithful Friend, and his excellency is invaluable.

{16} Chap 6 A Faithful Friend

[6:16-17] A faithful friend is the Medicine of Life; and they that fear the Lord shall find him.

Whoso feareth the Lord shall direct his friendship aright: for as he is, so shall his neighbour be also.

[7:18] Change not a friend for any good by no means; neither a faithful brother for the Gold of Ophir.

[7:20-21] Whereas thy servant worketh truly, entreat him not Evil, nor the hireling that bestoweth himself wholly for Thee.

Let thy Soul love a good Servant, and defraud him not of liberty.

{17} Seek Wisdom betimes. It is grievous to some

[6:18] My Son, gather instruction from thy Youth up: so shalt thou find Wisdom till thine old age.

[6:20-24] [[Wisdom is]] unpleasant to the unlearned: he that is without understanding will not remain with her.

She will lie upon him as a mighty Stone of trial; and he will cast her from him ere it be long.

For Wisdom is according to her name, and she is not manifest unto many.

Give ear, my Son, receive my Advice, and refuse not my Counsel,

and put thy feet into her fetters, and thy neck into her Chain.

{18} Chap 6 the fruits of Wisdom are pleasant
[6:25-30] Bow down thy shoulder, and bear her, and be not grieved with her Bonds.

Come unto her with thy whole heart, and keep her ways with all thy power.

Search, and seek, and she shall be made known unto thee: and when thou hast got hold of her, let her not go.

For at the last thou shalt find her rest, and that shall be turned to thy Joy.

Then shall her fetters be a strong defence for thee, and her Chains a robe of Glory.

For there is a [[robe of glory]] upon her, and her bands are purple lace.

{19} Be ready to hear Wise Men
[6:31-33] Thou shalt put her on, as a robe of honour, and shalt put her about thee as a Crown of Joy.

My Son, if thou wilt, thou shalt be taught: and if thou wilt apply thy mind, thou shalt be prudent.

If thou love to hear, thou shalt receive understanding: and if thou bow thine ear, thou shalt be wise.

[6:36-37] And if thou seest a Man of Understanding, get thee betimes unto him, and let thy foot wear the Steps of his door.

Let thy mind be upon the ordinances of the Lord, and meditate continually in his Commandments: he shall establish thine heart, and give thee Wisdom at thine own desire.

{20} Chap 7 to esteem a Friend, a Servant etc.
[7:1-3] Do no evil, so shall no harm come unto Thee.

Depart from the unjust, and [iniquity shall turn away from thee.

My Son] sow not upon the furrows of unrighteousness, and thou shalt not reap them sevenfold.

[7:9,14] Say not, God will look upon the multitude of my oblations.... .... and make not much babbling when thou prayest.

[7:11] Laugh no man to scorn in the bitterness of his Soul: for there is one which humbleth and exalteth.

[7:13] Use not to make any manner of lie: for the custom thereof is not good.

[7:12] Devise not a lie against thy brother; neither do the like to thy friend.

{21} the poor, and those that mourn
[7:34-35] Fail not to be with them that Weep, and mourn with them that mourn.

Be not slow to visit the Sick: for that shall make thee to be beloved.

[7:32] And stretch thine hand unto the poor, that thy blessing may be perfected.

[7:36] Whatsoever thou takest in hand, remember the end, and thou shalt never do amiss.

[9:18] A man of an ill Tongue is dangerous in his City; and he that is rash in his Talk shall be Hated.

[9:13] Keep thee far from the Man that hath power to kill; [so shalt thou not doubt the fear of death:] and if Thou come unto Him, make no fault, lest he take away thy Life presently: Remember that Thou goest in the midst of snares, and that thou walkest upon the Battlements of the City.

{22} Chap 8 Whom we may not strive with
[8:1-4] Strive not with a mighty Man, lest thou fall into his hands.

Be not at variance with a rich Man, lest he overweigh thee: for Gold hath destroyed many, and perverted the hearts of Kings.

Strive not with a Man that is full of tongue, and heap not wood upon his fire. 4Jest not with a rude man, lest thy ancestors be disgraced.

[8:11] Rise not up in Anger at the presence of an injurious person, lest he lie in wait to entrap thee in thy Words.

[8:10] Kindle not the Coals of a Sinner, lest thou be burnt with the flame of his Fire.

{23} nor provoke, nor have to do with

[8:12-14] Lend not unto him that is mightier than thyself; for if thou lendest him, count it but lost.

Be not surety above thy power: [for if thou be surety, take care to pay it.]

Go not to law with a Judge; for they will judge for him according to his honour.

[8:16] Strive not with an angry Man, and go not with him into a Solitary place: for Blood is as nothing in his sight, and where there is no help, he will overthrow thee.

[8:15] Travel not by the way with a bold fellow, lest he become grievous unto thee: for he will do according to his own will, and thou shalt perish with him, through his folly.

{24} Chap 8 Open not thy heart to every one
[8:17-19] Consult not with a Fool; for he cannot keep Counsel.

Do no secret thing before a Stranger; for thou knowest not what he will bring forth.

Open not thine heart to every Man, lest he requite thee with a shrewd turn.

[8:7] Rejoice not over thy greatest Enemy being dead, but remember that we die all.

[8:6] Dishonour not a Man in his Old Age: for even some of us wax old.

[8:9] Miss not the discourse of the Elders: for they also learned of their Fathers, and of them thou shalt learn understanding, and to give answer as need requireth.

{25} Know our Neighbours and converse with wise men Chap 9

[9:11-14] Envy not the glory of a Sinner: for thou knowest not what shall be his end.

Delight not in the thing that the ungodly have pleasure in; but remember they shall not go unpunished unto their Grave.

Keep thee far from the Man that hath power to kill; so shalt thou not doubt the fear of death: and if thou come unto him, make no fault, lest he take away thy life presently: remember that thou goest in the midst of Snares, and that thou walkest upon the Battlements of the City

As near as thou canst, guess at thy Neighbour, and consult with the Wise.

{26} Chap 10 the inconveniences and folly of pride

[9:18] A man of an ill Tongue is dangerous in his City; and he that is rash in his Talk shall be Hated[114].

[10:7] Pride is hateful before God and man...

[10:9] Why is Earth and Ashes proud?....

[10:12-13] The beginning of pride is when one departeth from God, and his heart is turned away from his Maker.

[10:13] [For] pride is the beginning of Sin...

[10:18] [Pride] was not made for men, nor furious Anger for them that are born of a Woman.

11:14-15] Prosperity and Adversity, life and death, poverty and riches, come of the Lord.

Wisdom, Knowledge, and understanding of the Law, are of the Lord: Love, and the...

{27} Wealth and all things else are from God ...way of good works, are from Him.

[11:19] whereas he saith, I have found rest, and now will eat continually of my goods; and *yet* he knoweth not what time shall come upon him, and that he must leave those things to others, and die.

[11:12] Again, there is another that is slow, and hath need of help, wanting ability, and full of

---

[114] Lord C is presumably unaware that he has already noted verses 13 & 18 on p. 21

poverty; yet the eye of the Lord looked upon him for Good, and set him up from his low estate.

[11:21] [Marvel not at the works of sinners; but] [[Therefore]] trust in the Lord, and abide in thy labour: for it is an easy thing in the sight of the Lord on the sudden to make a poor man rich.

[11:26] .. it is an easy thing [[for]] the Lord [in the day of death] to reward a man according to his ways.

{28} Chap 10 the commodities of a Wise Ruler
[10:2-3] As the Judge of the people is himself, so are his Officers; and what manner of Man the Ruler of the City is, such are all they that dwell therein.

[An unwise king destroyeth his people; but] [[and]] through the prudence of them which are in authority the City shall be inhabited.

[10:21] The fear of the Lord goeth before the obtaining of Authority: but roughness and pride are the losing thereof.

[10:6] Bear not hatred to thy Neighbour for every wrong; and do nothing at all by injurious practices.

{29} nor meddle with many matters[115]

[11:1-2] Wisdom lifteth up the Head of him that is of low degree, and maketh him to sit among great Men.

Commend not a Man for his Beauty; Neither abhor a Man for his outward appearance.

[11:7-9] Blame not before thou hast examined the truth: Understand first, and then rebuke.

Answer not before thou hast heard the Cause: neither interrupt Men in the midst of their Talk.

Strive not in a matter that concerneth thee not; and sit not in judgment with Sinners.

{30} Chap 11 bring not every Man into thy House

[11:25] In the day of prosperity there is a forgetfulness of Affliction: and in the day of Affliction there is no more remembrance of prosperity.

[11:27] The affliction of an hour maketh a Man forget pleasure: and in his end his deeds shall be discovered.

[11:29-31] Bring not every Man into thine House: for the deceitful man hath many trains.

---

[115] 11:10 'My son, meddle not with many matters', but Lord C. does not note the verse

[[and]] like as a [partridge taken and kept in a cage, so is the heart of the proud; and like as a] spy, watcheth he for thy fall:

for he lieth in wait, and turneth Good into Evil, and in things worthy praise will lay blame upon thee.

[11:33] Take heed of a Mischievous Man, for he worketh wickedness; lest he bring upon thee a perpetual Blot.

{31} be not liberal to the ungodly
[11:34] Receive a stranger into thine house, and he will disturb thee, and turn thee out of thine own.

[12:1-2] When thou wilt do good, know to whom thou doest it; so shalt thou be thanked for thy Benefits.

Do good to the Godly Man, and thou shalt find a recompense; and if not from him, yet from the most High.

[12:5] Do well unto him that is lowly, but give not to the ungodly: [hold back thy bread, and give it not unto him, lest he overmaster thee thereby:] for else thou shalt receive twice as much Evil for all the Good thou shalt have done unto him.

{32} Chap 12 Trust not thine Enemy

[12:8-11] A friend cannot be known in prosperity: and an enemy cannot be hidden in adversity.

In the prosperity of a man, enemies will be grieved: but in his Adversity even a Friend will depart.

Never trust thine enemy: [for like as iron rusteth, so is his wickedness]

Though he humble himself, and go crouching, yet take good heed and beware of him, and thou shalt be unto him as if thou hadst wiped a looking-glass, and thou shalt know that his rust hath not been altogether wiped away.

[12:15] For a while he will abide with thee, but if thou begin to fall, he will not tarry.

{33} ...nor the wicked

[12:12-14] Set him not by thee, lest, when he hath overthrown thee, he stand up in thy place; neither let him sit at thy right hand, lest he seek to take thy seat, and thou at the last remember my words, and be prick'd therewith.

Who will pity a charmer that is bitten with a Serpent, or any such as come nigh wild Beasts?

So one that goeth to a Sinner, and is defiled with him in his Sins, who will pity?

[12:17} If Adversity come upon thee, thou shalt find him there first; and though he pretend to help thee, yet shall he undermine thee.

{34} Chap 13 Keep not company with the proud

[12:16] An Enemy speaketh sweetly with his lips, but in his heart he imagineth how to throw thee into a pit: he will weep with his Eyes, but if he find opportunity, he will not be satisfied with Blood.

[13:1-2] [He that toucheth pitch shall be defiled therewith; and] he that hath fellowship with a proud man shall be like unto him.

Burden not thyself above thy power while thou livest; and have no fellowship with one that is mightier and richer than thyself...

[13;15-16] Every Beast loveth his like, and every man loveth his Neighbour.

All Flesh consorteth according to kind, and a Man will cleave to his like.

{35} difference between the Rich and the poor

[13:17-20] What fellowship hath the Wolf with the Lamb? so the Sinner with the Godly.

What agreement is there between the Hyena and a Dog? and what peace between the Rich and the poor?

As the Wild Ass is the Lion's prey in the Wilderness: so the Rich eat up the poor.

As the proud hate humility: so doth the rich abhor the poor.

[13:3-4] The rich Man hath done wrong, and yet he threateneth withal: the poor is wronged, and he must intreat also.

If thou be for his profit, he will use thee: but if thou have nothing, he will forsake thee.

{36} Chap 13 Keep not company with a Mightier than thy self

[13:5-8] If thou have any thing, he will live with thee: Yea, he will make thee bare, and will not be sorry for it.

If he have need of thee, he will deceive thee, and smile upon thee, and put thee in hope; he will speak thee fair, and say, what wantest Thou?

And he will shame thee by his meats, until he have drawn thee dry twice or thrice, and at the last he will laugh thee to scorn: Afterward, when he seeth thee, he will forsake thee, and shake his head at thee.

Beware that thou be not deceived, and brought down in thy Jollity.

{37}

[13:9-12] If thou be invited of a mighty Man, withdraw thyself, and so much the more will he invite thee.

press thou not upon him, lest thou be put back; stand not far off, lest thou be forgotten.

Affect not to be made equal unto him in talk, and believe not his many words: for with much communication will he tempt thee, and smiling upon thee will get out thy Secrets:

But cruelly he will lay up thy words, and will not spare to do thee hurt, and to put thee in prison.

{38} Chap 13 difference between the Rich and the poor

[13:13-14] Observe, and take good heed, for thou walkest in peril of thy overthrowing: when thou hearest these things, awake in thy sleep.

Love the Lord all thy life, and call upon him for thy Salvation.

[13:22] When a rich Man is fallen, he has many helpers: he speaketh things not to be spoken, and yet Men justify him: the poor man slipped, and [[yet]] they rebuked him [[too]]; he spake wisely, and could have no place.

[Proverbs 18:23] The poor useth entreaties; but the Rich answereth roughly.

{39} A Man's Heart will change his countenance
[13:23, 25-26] When a Rich man speaketh, every Man holdeth his Tongue, and, look, what he saith, they extol it to the Clouds: but if the poor Man speak, they say, what fellow is this? and if he stumble, they will help to overthrow him.

The Heart of a Man changeth his Countenance, whether it be for Good or Evil: and a Merry Heart maketh a chearful Countenance.

A [[merry]] Countenance is a token of a heart that is in prosperity...

[Proverbs 15:1]
A soft answer turneth away Wrath*:* but Grievous Words stir up Anger.

{40} Chap 14 A Good Conscience maketh Men Happy
[14:1-2) Blessed is the Man .... whose Conscience hath not Condemned him, and who is not fallen from his Hope in the Lord.

[14:11-15] My Son, according to thy Ability do good to thy Self, and give the Lord his due offering.

Remember that Death will not be long in coming, and that the Covenant of the Grave is not shewed unto thee.

Do good unto thy Friend before thou die, and according to thy Ability stretch out thy hand and give to him.

Defraud not thyself of the Good Day, and let not the part of a good desire overpass Thee.

{41} Do Thou Good
[14:15-17] Shalt thou not leave thy Travails unto another? and thy labours to be divided by lot?

Give, and take, and sanctify thy Soul; for there is no seeking of dainties in the Grave.

All Flesh waxeth Old as a Garment: for the Covenant from the beginning is, Thou shalt die the death.

[Horace, *Carmen Saeculare*, I. 4. 17] With equal pace, impartial Fate,

Knocks at the palace, as the Cottage Gate.
Horace

[Dacier] Let us reckon the Moments, Hours, Days, Months and Years of Life, and how inconsiderable is the Sum Total? [116]

{42} Chap 18 Wisdom embraceth those that Fear God

[15:1, 5-7] He that feareth the Lord will do good...

[[and Wisdom]] shall exalt him above his neighbours, and in the midst of the Congregation shall she open his Mouth.

He shall find Joy and a Crown of Gladness, and she shall cause him to inherit an Everlasting Name.

But Foolish men shall not attain unto her, and Sinners shall not see her.

[15:11-12] Say not Thou, It is through the Lord that I fell away: for thou oughtest not to do the things that he hateth.

---

[116] Lord C. has added the quote from Horace. The translation is by the Irish clergyman, Rev Philip Francis (1708-1773), and was published in 1741 when he was curate at St Peter's Dublin. Francis added this footnote to Horace's *vitae summa brevis,* which he attributes to the French classical scholar, Anne Dacier (1647-1720), though curiously he seems unaware that Anne Dacier was a woman, referring to her as 'Mr Dacier'.

Say not Thou, he hath caused me to err: for he hath no need of a Sinful Man.

{43} We may not Charge God with our Faults
[15:13-18] The Lord hateth all Abomination: and they that Fear God love it not.

He himself made Man from the beginning, and left him in the hand of his Counsel;

If thou wilt, to keep the Commandments, and to perform acceptable Faithfulness.

He hath set Fire and Water before Thee: stretch forth thy hand unto whether thou wilt.

Before Man is Life and Death; and whether him liketh shall be given him.

For the Wisdom of the Lord is great, and he is mighty in power, and beholdeth all things:

{44} Chap 18 Do not Blemish thy good deeds with ill Words
[15:20] He hath commanded no Man to do Wickedly, neither hath he given any Man License to Sin.

[18-15-16] My son, blemish not thy good deeds, neither use uncomfortable words when thou givest any thing.

Shall not the dew assuage the heat? so is a word better than a gift.

[18:25] When thou hast enough, remember the time of Hunger: and when thou art rich, think upon poverty and Need.

[18:30] Go not after thy Lusts, but refrain thyself from thine Appetites.

{45} Follow not thy pleasures to excess
[18:31] If thou givest thy Soul the desires that please her, she will make thee a laughing Stock to thine Enemies that Malign thee.

[18:33] Be not made a Beggar by banqueting upon borrowing, when thou hast nothing in thy purse: for thou shalt lie in wait for thine own life, and be talked on.

[19:1] ... He that contemneth small things shall fall by little and little.

[19:4] ... He that is hasty to give Credit is light minded;

[19:6] He that can Rule his Tongue shall live without Strife; and he that hateth Babbling shall have less Evil.

{46} Chap 19 Say not all thou hearest
[19:7-8] Rehearse not unto another that which is told unto thee, and thou shalt fare never the worse.

Whether it be to Friend or Foe, talk not of other men's lives...

[19:10-11] ... if thou hast heard a word, let it die with thee; and be bold, it will not burst thee.

A Fool travaileth with a Word, as a Woman in Labour of a Child.

[19:16] There is one that slippeth in his speech, but not from his heart; and who is he that hath not offended with his Tongue?

[19:30] A Man's Attire, and excessive Laughter, [and gait,] show what he is.

{47} Of Silence and Speaking. Chap 20

[20:2-3] It is much better to reprove, than to be angry secretly: and he that confesseth his fault shall be preserved from hurt.

How good is it, when thou art reproved, to show repentance! for so shalt thou escape wilful sin.

[20:8] He that useth many Words shall be abhorred; and he that taketh to himself Authority therein shall be hated.

[20:13] [[But]] A wise man by his words maketh him beloved..

[20:14] The Gift of a Fool shall do thee no good when thou hast it; neither yet of the envious for his necessity: for he looketh to receive many Things for One.

{48} Chap. 20 Of slipping by the Tongue
[20:15] He giveth little, and upbraideth much; he openeth his mouth like a Crier; to day he lendeth, and tomorrow will he ask it again: such a one is to be hated of God and Man.

[20:18] ...To slip upon a pavement is better than to slip with the Tongue...

[20:19-20] An unprofitable[117] Tale will always be in the Mouth of the Unwise.

A wise Sentence shall be rejected when it cometh out of a Fool's Mouth; for he will not speak it in due season.

[20:29] Presents and Gifts blind the Eyes of the Wise, and stop up his Mouth that he cannot reprove.

{49} Flee from Sin as from a Serpent Chap 21
[20:30] Wisdom that is hid, and Treasure that is hoarded up, what profit is in them both.

[21:1-4] My Son, hast thou sinned? do so no more, but ask pardon for thy former Sins.

---

[117] The KJV has 'unseasonable'.

Flee from Sin as from the face of a Serpent: for if thou comest too near it, it will bite thee: the teeth thereof are as the teeth of a lion, slaying the souls of men.

All iniquity is as a two-edged Sword, the wounds whereof cannot be healed.

To terrify and do wrong will waste Riches: thus the House of proud Men shall be made desolate.

{50} Chap 22. Meddle not with Fools
[22:13] ... Go not to him that hath no Understanding: Beware of him, lest thou have trouble, and thou shalt never be defiled with his fooleries: depart from him, and thou shalt find rest, and never be disquieted with madness.

[22:15-16] Sand, and Salt, and a Mass of Iron, is easier to bear, than a Man without Understanding.

As Timber girt and bound together in a Building cannot be loosed with shaking: so the heart that is stablished by advised Counsel shall fear at no time.

[22:22] If thou hast opened thy mouth against thy Friend, fear not; for there may be a reconciliation: except for upbraiding, or pride, or...

{51} What will lose a Friend

...disclosing of Secrets, or a treacherous Wound: for, for these things every Friend will depart.

[23:1] O Lord, Father and Governor of all my whole life, leave me not to their Counsels, and let me not fall by them.

[23:2] [[Set]]the discipline of Wisdom over mine heart [that they spare me not for mine ignorances, and it pass not by my sins]

Lest mine ignorances increase, and my sins abound to my destruction, and I fall before mine Adversaries, and mine Enemy rejoice over me, whose hope is far from thy mercy.

"Give me strength to bear the Burthern thy providence has appointed and deliver me from Fear and a peevish fretful Mind"[118].

{52} Chap 23 A prayer for Grace etc
[23:4-5] O Lord, Father and Governor[119] of my [[whole]] Life, give me not a proud look, but

---

[118] I haven't been able to source this prayer. It is similar to the prayers found in books of prayers for domestic use that were in circulation at this time, and it fits the tone of the quotations from Ecclesiasticus ch.23.
[119] The KJV has 'God'.

turn away from thy servants always a haughty mind.

Turn away from me vain hopes and concupiscence, and thou shalt hold him up that is desirous always to serve thee.

[23:9-10] Accustom not thy mouth to swearing; neither use thyself to the naming of the Holy One.

For [as a servant that is continually beaten shall not be without a blue mark: so] he that sweareth and nameth God continually shall not be faultless.

[23:15] The Man that is accustomed to opprobrious Words will never be reformed all the days of his life.

{53} 3 sorts of Sins

[23:16-19] Two sorts of Men multiply Sin, and the third will bring Wrath: a Hot Mind is as a Burning Fire, it will never be quenched till it be consumed: a fornicator [in the body of his flesh] will never cease till he hath kindled a fire.

[All bread is sweet to a whoremonger,] [[and]]he will not leave off till he die.

A man that breaketh Wedlock, saying thus in his heart, Who seeth me? I am compassed about with darkness, the Walls cover me, and no body seeth me; What need I to fear? The most High will not remember my Sins:

such a man only feareth the Eyes of Men, and knoweth not that the Eyes of the Lord are ten thousand times brighter than the Sun, beholding all the ways of Men...

{54} Chap 25 What things are beautiful
[23:21-22] This man shall be punished in the Streets of the City, and where he suspecteth not he shall be taken.

Thus shall it go also with the Wife that leaveth her Husband, and bringeth in an Heir by another.

[25:1] [Three things are beautiful, both before God and men][120]:

The Unity of Brethren,

The love of Neighbours,

A Man and a Wife that agree together.

{55} ... and what have fruit
[25:2]Three sorts of Men my Soul Hateth, and I am greatly offended at their Life:

A poor Man that is proud,

---

[120] The KJV has "In Three things I was beautified, and stood up beautiful"

A rich Man that is a Liar,

And an old Adulterer that doteth.

[25:3-5] If thou hast gathered nothing in thy Youth, How canst Thou find any thing in thine Age?

O how comely a thing is Judgment for Gray Hairs, and for Ancient Men to know Council!

Much experience is the Crown of Old Men, and the Fear of God is their Glory.

{56} Chap 25 Nothing worse than a Wicked Woman

[25:13-17] Give me any plague, but the plague of the Heart: And any Wickedness, but the Wickedness of a Woman:

And any Affliction, but the Affliction from them that Hate me: And any Revenge, but the Revenge of Enemies.

[There is no head above the head of a serpent; and] There is no Wrath above the Wrath of an Enemy.

I had rather live with a Lion and a Dragon, than to keep House with a Wicked Woman [[(or Man)]][121].

---

[121] It's strange that Lord C should have included any part of these misogynistic passages, since he is

The Wickedness of a Woman changeth her Face, and darkeneth her Countenance like Sackcloth.

{57}
[25:18] Her Husband shall sit among his Neighbours; and when he heareth it shall sigh Bitterly.

[25:23] A Wicked Woman abateth the Courage, maketh an heavy Countenance and a Wounded Heart: a Woman that will not comfort her Husband in distress maketh Weak Hands and Feeble Knees.

[25:20, 22, 21] As the Climbing of a Sandy Way is to the Feet of the Aged, so is a Wife full of Words to a quiet Man.

A Woman, if she maintain her Husband, is full of Anger, Impudence, and much reproach.

Stumble not at the Beauty of a woman, and desire her not for pleasure.

---

clearly unhappy wit the main part of them. I think that he never regarded his wife as wicked. He seems to have been humiliated by her behaviour during their marriage, but his later attitude was more one of regret at what might have been. His addition of "or Man" is a clumsy attempt to make the passage less objectionable.

{58} Chap 26 Three things that are grievous
[26:5] There be three things that mine heart feareth; [and for the fourth I was sore afraid:]
the slander of a city,
the gathering together of an unruly multitude,
and a false accusation: all these are worse than death.
[26:28] There be two things that grieve my heart; and the third maketh me Angry:
a Man of War that suffereth poverty;
And Men of Understanding that are not set by;
And one that returneth from righteousness to Sin; [the Lord prepareth such an one for the sword.]
[27:22-23} He that winketh with the Eyes worketh Evil: And he that knoweth him will depart from him.
When thou art present, he will speak sweetly, and will admire thy Words: but at the last he will writhe his Mouth, and slander thy Sayings.

{59} Backbiting Chap 28
[28:9] A Sinful Man disquieteth Friends, and maketh debate among them that be at peace.

[28:14] A b

A Backbiting Tongue hath disquieted many, and driven them from Nation to Nation: Strong

Cities hath it pulled down, and overthrown the Houses of great Men.

[28:16-19] Whoso hearkeneth unto it shall never find rest, and never dwell quietly.

The stroke of the Whip maketh marks in the Flesh: But the stroke of the Tongue breaketh the Bones.

Many have fallen by the edge of the Sword: but not so many as have fallen by the Tongue.

Well is he that [is defended from it, and] hath not passed through the venom of it.

{60} Chap 29 We must shew mercy
[29:10] [Lose thy money for thy brother and thy friend, and] Let not [[thy money]] rust under a stone to be lost.

Lay up thy Treasure according to the Commandments of the most High, and it shall bring Thee more profit than Gold.

Shut up Alms in thy Store Houses: and it shall deliver thee from all Affliction.

It shall Fight for Thee against thine Enemies better than a Mighty Shield and strong Spear.

[31:8-9] Blessed is the Rich that is found without blemish, And hath not gone after Gold.

Who is he? and we will call him blessed: for wonderful things hath he done among his people.

{61} Health is better than Wealth. Chap 30
[30:16-20] There is no Riches above a Sound Body, and no Joy above the Joy of the Heart.

Death is better than a bitter life or continual sickness.

Delicates poured upon a Mouth shut up are as Messes of Meat set upon a Grave.

What Good doeth the Offering unto an Idol? for neither can it eat nor smell: so is he that is persecuted of the Lord.

He only Seeth with his Eyes and groaneth [as an eunuch that embraceth a virgin] and sigheth[122].

[31:2] Watching Care will not let a Man Slumber, as a sore disease breaketh Sleep.

{62} Chap 30 Health and Life are shortened by Grief
[30:21-24] Give not over thy Mind to Heaviness, and Afflict not thyself in thine own Counsel.

The Gladness of the Heart is the life of man, and the joyfulness of a Man prolongeth his days.

---

[122] Lord C generally omits any mention of eunuchs!

Love thine own Soul, and Comfort thy heart, remove sorrow far from thee: for Sorrow hath killed many, and there is no profit therein.

Envy and Wrath shorten the Life, and carefulness bringeth Age before the time.

[Proverbs 15:15]
All the days of the afflicted are Evil: But he that is of a merry heart hath a Continual Feast.

{63} Chap. 32
[32:7-10] Speak, Young Man, if there be need of thee: [and yet scarcely when thou art twice asked.]

[[But]] let thy Speech be short, comprehending much in few Words; be as one that knoweth and yet holdeth his Tongue.

If thou be among great Men, make not thyself equal with them; And when Ancient Men are in place, use not many Words.

Before the Thunder goeth Lightning; and before a shamefaced Man shall go Favour.

[32:17-18] A sinful Man will not be reproved, but findeth an excuse according to his Will.

A man of council will be considerate; But a [strange and] proud Man is not daunted with

Fear, even when of himself he hath done without Council.

{64} Chap. 33. Chiefly regard thyself
[32:19] Do nothing without Advice; and when Thou hast once done, repent not.

[33:4] Prepare what to say, and so thou shalt be heard…

[33:19-22] Give not thy Son [and] Wife, thy Brother and Friend, power over Thee while thou livest, and give not thy Goods to another: lest it repent Thee, and thou intreat for the same again.

As long as thou livest and hast breath in thee, give not thyself over to any.

For better it is that thy Children should seek [to] Thee, Than that thou shouldest stand to their Courtesy.

In all thy works keep to thyself [the] pre-eminence; leave not a stain in thine Honour.

{65} the Blessing of them that Fear the Lord. Chap 34
[Proverbs 16:32]
He that is slow to Anger is better than the Mighty; and he that Ruleth his Spirit than he that taketh a City.

[34:1] The Hopes of a Man void of Understanding are Vain and false: and dreams lift up Fools.

[34:14] He that feareth the Lord shall not [fear nor] be afraid; for he is his Hope.

[34:16-17] For the Eyes of the Lord are upon them that Love him, he is their mighty protection and strong stay, a defence from heat, and a Cover from the Sun at Noon, a preservation from stumbling, and an help from falling.

He raiseth up the Soul, and lighteneth the Eyes: He giveth Health, Life, and Blessing.

{66} Chap. 34 the Sacrifices of the Wicked not pleasing to God

[34:18-22] He that sacrificeth of a thing wrongfully gotten, his Offering is Ridiculous; and the Gifts of unjust Men are not accepted.

The most High is not pleased with the offerings of the Wicked; neither is he pacified for Sin by the multitude of Sacrifices.

Whoso bringeth an offering of the Goods of the poor doeth as one that killeth the Son before his Father's Eyes.

The Bread of the Needy is their Life: he that defraudeth them thereof is a Man of Blood.

He that taketh away his Neighbour's living slayeth him; And he that defraudeth the Labourer of his Hire is a Blood-shedder.

{67} Chap 35

[34:23] When one Buildeth, and Another pulleth down, what profit have they then but Labour?

[34:26] [So is it with] A man that Fasteth for his Sins, and goeth again, and doeth the same: Who will hear his prayer? Or what doth his humbling profit him?

[35:3] To depart from Wickedness is a Thing pleasing to the Lord; and to forsake unrighteousness is a propitiation.

[35:7] The Sacrifice of a just Man is acceptable. and the Memorial thereof shall never be forgotten.

[35:12] Do not think to corrupt with Gifts; for such he will not receive: and Trust not to unrighteous Sacrifices; for the Lord is Judge, and with him is no respect of persons.

{68} Chap. 37. How to know Friends and Counsellors

[35:19] [[The Lord will render]]to every Man according to his deeds, and to the works of Men according to their devices; till he have judged the Cause of his people, and made them to rejoice in his Mercy.

[37:1-2] Every Friend saith, I am his Friend also: But there is a Friend, which is only a Friend in Name.

Is it not a grief unto death, when a Companion and Friend is turned to an Enemy?

[37:4] There is a Companion, which rejoiceth in the prosperity of a Friend, but in the time of trouble will be against him.

[27:24] I have hated many things, but nothing like him, fore the Lord will hate him.

{69} Consult only with a Wise Man

[37:8-11] Beware of a Counsellor, and know before what need he hath; for he will Counsel for himself; lest he cast the lot upon Thee,

and say unto Thee, Thy way is good: and afterward he stand on the other side, to see what shall befall thee.

Consult not with one that suspecteth Thee: and hide thy Counsel from such as Envy Thee.

Neither consult with a Woman touching her of whom [[she is]] jealous;

Neither with a Coward in matters of War;

Nor with a merchant concerning Exchange;

Nor with an unmerciful Man touching kindness;

Nor with a buyer of selling;

{70} Take Counsel of a Wise Man
[37:11-13] Nor with an envious Man, of Thankfulness;

Nor with an unmerciful Man, touching kindness;

Nor with the slothful, for any work; [nor with an hireling for a year of finishing work;]

Nor with an idle servant of much business: hearken not unto these in any matter of counsel.

But be continually with a Godly Man, whom thou knowest to keep the Commandments of the Lord, whose Mind is according to thy Mind, and will sorrow with Thee, if thou shalt miscarry.

And let the Counsel of thine own heart stand: For there is no Man more faithful unto thee than [[thy self]].

{71}
[37:14-16] For a Man's Mind is sometime wont to tell him more than seven Watchmen, that sit above in an high Tower.

But above all this pray to the most High, that he will direct thy way in Truth.

Let reason go before every enterprise, and Counsel before every Action.

[38:20] Take no heaviness to heart: drive it away, and remember the last end.

[38:18] For of heaviness cometh death, and the heaviness of the Heart breaketh Strength.

{72} Chap. 38. The Wisdom of Learned Men
[38:24-28] The Wisdom of a learned man cometh by opportunity of leisure: and he that hath little business shall become wise.

How can he get Wisdom that holdeth the plow, and that glorieth in the Goad, that driveth Oxen, and is occupied in their labours, and whose Talk is of Bullocks?

He giveth his mind to make Furrows; and is diligent to give the Kine Fodder.

So every Carpenter and workmaster, that laboureth Night and Day: [and they that cut and grave seals, and are diligent to make great variety, and give themselves to counterfeit imagery, and watch to finish a work:][123]

---

[123] It's understandable that Lord C omits this part of v. 27. Making counterfeit imagery doesn't measure

The Smith also sitting by the Anvil, and considering the Ironwork, the Vapour of the Fire wasteth his Flesh, and he fighteth with the Heat of the Furnace: the noise...

{73} And of the Labourer and Artificer, and the use of them both

[38:28-29] ...of the Hammer and the Anvil is ever in his ears, and his Eyes look still upon the pattern of the thing that he maketh; he setteth his mind to finish his work, and watcheth to polish it perfectly:

so doth the potter etc

[38:31-33] All these trust to their hands: and every one is wise in his work.

Without these cannot a City be inhabited: [and they shall not dwell where they will, nor go up and down:]

These shall not be sought for in publick Counsel, nor sit high in the Congregation: They shall not sit in the Judges' Seat, nor understand the Sentence of Judgment: [and they shall not be found where parables are spoken]

But they will maintain the State of the World, and all their desire is in the work of their Craft.

---

up against the other noble feats of labour.

{74} Chap 39
[37:19-20] There is one that is wise and teacheth many, and yet is unprofitable to himself.

There is one that showeth Wisdom in Words, and is hated...

[37:22-24] Another is Wise to himself; and the fruits of Understanding are commendable in his Mouth.

A wise man [[that]] instructeth his people; [and the fruits of his understanding fail not.

A wise man] shall be filled with blessing; and all they that see him shall count him happy.

[27:17-19, 20] Love thy Friend, and be faithful unto him: But if Thou hast betrayed him, follow no more after Him.

For as a Man hath destroyed his Enemy; So hast Thou lost the Love of thy Neighbour.

Follow after him no more, for he is too far off; he is [as a roe escaped out of the snare.][124]

---

[124] Lord C probably included the end of v. 20, but it was lost when the notebook was rebound and the pages trimmed. He also notes that the last three verses on p. 74 are from ch. 27. Though he doesn't mention that the other verses are from ch. 37, even though the heading is 'Chap 39'.

{75} Many Miseries in a Man's Life Chap. 40

[40:1-5] Great Travail is created for every Man, and an heavy Yoke is upon the Sons of Adam, from the day of their birth[125], till the day that they return to the Mother of all Things.

Their imagination of Things to come, and the Day of Death, trouble their Thoughts, and cause fear of Heart;

From him that sitteth on a Throne of Glory, unto him that is humbled in Earth and Ashes;

from him that weareth purple and a Crown, unto him that is clothed with a linnen Frock.

Wrath, and Envy, trouble, and unquietness, Fear of Death, Anger and strife, hinder [and in the time of rest upon his bed his night sleep, do change his knowledge][126]

{76} Chap. 41 The remembrance of death

[40:6-9] A little or nothing is his rest, and afterward he is in his sleep, as in a day of

---

[125] The text has "from the day that they go out of their mother's womb". Lord C prefers something with less anatomy!

[126] The rebinding process has cut off the last line in the book, which seems to be different from that given in the text.

keeping Watch, troubled in the vision of his heart, as if he were escaped out of a Battle.

When all is safe, he awaketh, and marveleth that the fear was nothing.

Such things happen unto all flesh, [both man and beast, and that is sevenfold more upon sinners]

[[And for the Wicked are Created]] Death, and Bloodshed, Strife, and Sword, Calamities, Famine, [tribulation,] and the scourge;[127]

[41:2] O Death, acceptable is thy Sentence unto the Needy, and unto him whose strength faileth, that is now in the last Age, and is vexed with all things, and to him that....

{77}
[41:2-4]... despaireth, and hath lost patience!

Fear not the Sentence of Death, remember them that have been before Thee, and that come after; for this is the Sentence of the Lord over all Flesh.

And why art thou against the pleasure of the most High? [there is no inquisition in the grave,

---

[127] Lord C has rearranged the text, using the opening of v. 10 'these things are created for the wicked' as his opening in v. 9 and omitting the end of v.8.

whether thou have lived ten, or an hundred, or a thousand years.][128]

[41:1] [[But]] O death, how bitter is the remembrance of thee to a Man that liveth at rest in his possessions, unto the Man that hath nothing to vex him, and that hath prosperity in all Things;

"But no pity for his victim Pluto knows" *Horace*[129]

{78} Horace [Odes Book 2:3 – to Quintus Dellius[130]]

Tho' You could Boast a Monarch's Birth;

Tho' wealth unbounded round thee flows;

---

[128] Interesting that Lord C omits the end of v. 4, in which the author shows that he has no faith in an after-life – in accordance with majority Jewish teaching at that time.

[129] We already encountered Philip Francis' translation of Horace on p. 41. This quote from one of the odes fits well on the theme of death's inevitability in ch. 41 of Ecclesiasticus, and sends Lord C back to the classics. The final chapters, where the author of Ecclesiasticus moves from Proverbs-style moral instruction to reflections on creation and on the story of the Jewish people were not so much to his taste.

[130] Quintus Dellius was a Roman soldier & politician – a late recruit to the side of Octavian (Augustus) in his struggle with Antony.

Tho' poor, and sprung from vulgar Earth,

No pity for his victim Pluto knows;

Thus all must tread the paths of Fate,

Thus ever shakes the mortal urn,

Whose lot embarks us, soon or late,

On Charon's Boat, ah! never to return.

It was customary among the Ancients to decide Affairs of the utmost consequence by Lot, they feigned that the Names of all Mankind were written upon Billets, and thrown into an Urn which was perpetually in motion; and that they whose Billets were first drawn should die first.[131]

{79} Horace [Odes Book 2:14- to Postumus - excerpts]

How swiftly fly the Winged Years!
For oh! Nor piety, nor Tears
Can stop the fleeting day;
Deep-furrowed wrinkles, posting Age,
And Death with irresistless Rage,
Are Strangers to delay.

---

[131] Anne Dacier's note on 'thus ever shakes the mortal urn' which Philip Francis quotes in his translation.

All Mortals tasting earthly Food,
Are doom'd to pass the joyless Flood,
And hear the Stygian Roar;
The sceptred King who rules the Earth,
The labouring Hind of humbler Birth,
Must reach the distant Shore.

Thy Cypress only, hated Tree,
Of all thy much-loved Groves, shall Thee,
Its short-liv'd Lord attend.

The Romans were passionately fond of Trees, ands curious in their Culture of them, that they often watered them, if such an expression may be allowed, with Wine....

{80}

..The Cypress was Sacred to Pluto and Proserpine, and various are the Reasons why it was used in Funerals: Either from a vulgar Error that it dies if it is pruned; or because it was useful in preserving a dead Body from corruption; or, being thrown into the Pyle, it corrected the offensive stench of the burning Carcase. A Branch of it was placed over the door of the House where any Person died, that the Pontiff might not be polluted by entering into it.[132]

---

[132] This was note in Francis' edition, attributed to a Mr Lamb. I've not been able to discover who Mr

{81} We must shew mercy and lend, but the Borrower must not defraud the lender.
Ecclesiasticus Chap. 29[133]
[29:4-7] Many, when a thing was lent them, reckoned it to be found, and put them to trouble that helped them.

Till he hath received, he will kiss a Man's hand; and for his neighbour's Money he will speak submissively: but when he should repay, He will prolong the time, and return Words of Grief, and complain of the Time.

If he prevail, he shall hardly receive the half, [and he will count as if he had found it:] If not, he hath deprived him of his money, And he hath gotten him an Enemy without Cause: He payeth Him with Cursings and Railings; and for Honour he will pay him disgrace.

Many therefore have refused to lend for other Men's ill-dealing, fearing to be defrauded.

The End of Ecclesiasticus – The Beginning of the Wisdom of Solomon

{82] Blank

Lamb was.

[133] This is not from the text of Ecclesiasticus, but a commentary at the beginning of the chapter on vv. 1-7

{83} The Wisdom of Solomon Chap 1st
[1:1-8] [Love righteousness, ye that be judges of the earth: think of the Lord with a good heart, and] In simplicity of heart seek [[the Lord]].

[For he will be found of them that tempt him not; and showeth himself unto such as do not distrust him.]

For Froward thoughts separate from God: and his power, when it is tried, reproveth the unwise.

For into a malicious soul wisdom shall not enter; [nor dwell in the body that is subject unto sin.]

For the Holy Spirit of discipline will Flee deceit, and remove from Thoughts that are without understanding, and will not abide when unrighteousness cometh in.

[For wisdom is a loving spirit; and will not acquit a blasphemer of his words:] for God is witness of his Reins, and a True Beholder of his Heart, and a Hearer of his Tongue.

For the Spirit of the Lord filleth the World: [and that which containeth all things hath knowledge of the voice.]

Therefore He that speaketh unrighteous things cannot be hid: neither shall vengeance....

{84} Chap 1st
[1:8-9] ...when it punisheth, pass by Him.

For inquisition shall be made into the Counsels of the ungodly: and the Sound of his Words shall come unto the Lord for the Manifestation of his wicked deeds.

[1:11-12] Therefore beware [of murmuring, which is unprofitable;] and refrain your Tongue from Backbiting: For there is no Word so Secret, that shall go for nought: and the Mouth that Belieth slayeth the Soul.

Seek not death in the Error of Your Life: and pull not upon Your Selves destruction with the works of your Hands.

{85} Meddle not with Fools Eccles Chap 22 v. 8
He that telleth a Tale to a Fool speaketh to one in a Slumber: When he hath told his Tale, He will say, What is the Matter?

[22:7] He that Teacheth a Fool is[as one that glueth a potsherd together, and] as he that waketh one from a sound Sleep – *Eccles.*

{86} Chap 2nd, Wisdom of Solomon
The wicked think this life is short, and of no other after this...

[1:1-4] For the ungodly said, reasoning with themselves, but not aright: Our life is short and tedious, and in the death of a Man there is no remedy: neither was there any man known to have returned from the Grave.

For we are born at all Adventure: And we shall be hereafter as though we had never been: for the Breath in Our Nostrils is as Smoke, and a little Spark in the moving of our Heart.

Which being extinguished, Our Body shall be turned into ashes, and our Spirit shall vanish as the Soft Air:

And our name shall be forgotten in Time, And no Man shall have Our Works in....

{87} ... therefore they will take their pleasure in This

[2:4, 6-10] ... Remembrance,
Come on therefore, let us enjoy the Good Things that are present: [and let us speedily use the creatures like as in youth.]
Let us fill Ourselves with Costly Wine, and Ointments: and let no Flower of the Spring pass by us.
Let us Crowne Ourselves with Rose-buds, before they be withered.
Let none of us go without his part of Voluptuousness: let us leave Tokens of our

joyfulness in every place: For this is Our portion, and our Lot is this.
Let us oppress the poor Righteous Man, Let us not spare the Widow, nor reverence the Ancient gray Hairs of the Aged.

{88} Chap 2nd The Wicked Conspire against the just

[2:11-12, 14-17] Let Our Strength be the Law of Justice: For that which is Feeble is found to be nothing worth.

Therefore let us lie in wait for the Righteous: Because he is not for our turn, [and he is clean contrary to our doings:] He upbraideth us with our offending the Law, and Objecteth to our infamy the transgressions of our Education.

He was made to reprove our Thoughts.

And he is grievous to us even to Behold: For his life is not like other Mens, his ways are of another fashion.

[We are esteemed of him as counterfeits: he abstaineth from our ways as from filthiness:] He pronounceth the end of the just to be Blessed, and maketh his boast that God is his Father.

Let us see if his words be true: and let us prove what shall happen in the end of him.

{89} The Wicked Conspire against the just
[2:18-19, 21-23] For if the just Man be the Son of God, he will help him, and deliver him from the hands of his Enemies.

Let us examine him with despitefulness and torture, That we may know his Meekness, and prove his patience.

Such Things they did imagine, and were deceived: For their own wickedness hath Blinded them.

As for the mysteries of God, they knew them not: Neither hoped they for the wages of Righteousnes: nor discerned a Reward for blameless Souls.

For God Created Man to be Immortal, and made him to be an Image of his own Eternity.

{90} Chap 3rd The Godly are Happy in their Death...
[3:1-6] [But] The souls of the Righteous are in the Hand of God, and there shall no Torment touch them.

In the Sight of the unwise they seemed to die: And their departure is taken for Misery,

And their going from us to be utter destruction: But they are in peace.

For though they bee punished in the Sight of Men: Yet is their Hope full of Immortality.

And having bene a little Chastised, they shall be greatly rewarded: For God proved them, and found them worthy for Himself.

As Gold in the Furnace hath he tried them, and received them as a burnt Offering.

{91} ... and in their Troubles: The Wicked are not.
[3:10-12] But the Ungodly shall be punished according to their own imaginations, which have neglected the Righteous, and Forsaken the Lord.

For whoso despiseth Wisdom, and Nurture, he is miserable, and their hope is Vain, their labours unfruitful, and their Works unprofitable.

Their Wives are Foolish, and their Children Wicked.

For though they live long, yet shall they be nothing regarded: And their last Age shall be without Honour.

Or if they die quickly, they have no Hope, [neither comfort in the day of trial.]

For Horrible is the End of the unrighteous Generation.

{92} the Just die young and are Happy

[4:7-11] But though the Righteous be prevented with death: Yet shall he be at Rest.

For honourable Age is not that which standeth in length of Time, nor that is measured by number of Years.

But wisdom is the Gray Hair unto Men, & an unspotted Life is Old Age.

He pleased God, and was beloved of Him: So that living amongst Sinners, he was translated.

Yea, speedily was he taken away, lest that Wickedness should alter his Understanding, Or deceit beguile his Soul.

{93} The Wicked shall confess their Error, and the vanity of their Lives

[5:1, 3-4, 6] The Righteous Man shall stand in great boldnes, before the Face of such as have Afflicted him, and made no account of his Labours.

And they repenting, and groaning for Anguish [of spirit], shall say within themselves, This was he whom we had sometimes in derision, and a proverb of reproach.

We Fools accounted his life Madness, and his End to be without Honour.

Therefore have we erred from the way of Truth, and the Light of Righteousness hath not shined unto us, and the Sun of Righteousness rose not upon us.

{94} Chap 5th God will reward the Just...
[5:7-10] We wearied Ourselves in the way of wickedness, and destruction: Yea, we have gone through deserts, where there lay no Way: but as for the way of the Lord, we have not known it.

What has pride profited us? Or what good has Riches with our Vaunting brought us?

All Those Things are passed away like a Shadow, and as a post that hasted by.

And as a Ship that passeth over the Waves of the Water, which when it is gone by, The Trace thereof cannot be found: neither the pathway of the Keel in the Waves.

{95} ... And War against the Wicked
[5:14-17] For the Hope of the Ungodly is like dust that is blowen away with the Wind, [like a thin froth that is driven away with the storm:] and as a Smoke which is dispersed here and

there with a Tempest, and passeth away as the remembrance of a Guest that tarrieth but a day.

But the Righteous lie for Evermore, [their reward also is with the Lord], and the Care of Them is with the most High.

[Therefore shall they receive a glorious kingdom, & a beautiful crown from the Lords hand:] For with his right hand shall he cover them, and with his Arm shall he protect Them.

He shall take to him his jealous for complete Armour, & make the Creature His Weapon for the revenge of his Enemies.

{96} Chap. 5th. God will war against the Wicked
[5:18-22] He shall put on Righteousness as a Breast plate, and true Judgement instead of an Helmet.

He shall take Holiness for an Invincible Shield.

His severe wrath shall he sharpen for a Sword, and the World shall Fight with him against the Wicked.

Then shall the right-aiming Thunder Bolts go abroad, and from the Clouds, as from a well-drawn Bow,[shall they fly to the mark.]

[And hailstones full of wrath shall be cast as out of a stonebow,] and the Water of the Sea shall

Rage against Them, & the Floods shall cruelly drown Them.

{97} Chap. 6th Princes and Great Men have their power from God, who will not spare Them

[6:1, 3-5] Hear therefore, O ye Kings, and understand, Hear ye that be judges of the ends of the Earth.

For power is given You of the Lord, & sovereignty from the Highest, who shall try your Works; and search out your Counsels.

Because being Ministers of his Kingdom, you have not judged aright, nor kept the Law, nor walked after the Counsel of God,

Horribly and speedily shall he come upon You: for a sharp Judgement shall be to Them that be in High places.

{97}[134] Chap. 6th. Kings have their power from God

[6:6-7, 9] For mercy will soon pardon the Meanest: But Mighty Men shall be mightily tormented.

For He which is Lord over All, shall Fear no Mans person: neither shall He Stand in Awe of any

---

[134] Lord C has given two pages the number '97'.

Mans Greatness: For He hath made the Small and Great, and Careth for all alike.

Unto You therefore, O Kings, doe I speak, that you may learn Wisdom, and not fall away.

[6:21] If your delight be in Thrones and Scepters, O ye Kings of the people, Honour Wisdom that ye may Reign for Evermore.

{98} Wisdom is soon Found

[6:12-14, 16] Wisdom is Glorious and never Fadeth Away: Yea she is easily seen of them that love her, and found of such as seek Her.

She preventeth them that desire her, in making Herself first known unto them.

Whoso seeketh her early, shall have no great Travail: for he shall find her sitting at his doors.

For she goeth about seeking such as are worthy of Her, sheweth herself favourably unto them in the ways, and meeteth them in every Thought.

[6:24] But the Multitude of the Wise is the Welfare of the World: and a Wise King is the upholding of the people.

{99} Chap. 8th. He that hath Wisdom hath every good thing

[8:7-9] [And if a man love Righteousness, her labours are virtues: for she] Wisdom teacheth

Temperance and prudence: Justice and Fortitude, which are such Things as men can have nothing more profitable in their Life.

If a Man desire much experience: She knoweth Things of Old, and Conjectureth Aright what is to Come: She knoweth the Subtleties of Speeches, and can expound dark Sentences: She foreseeth Signs [and wonders], and the Events of Seasons and Times.

Therefore I purposed to take her to me to live with me, knowing that she would be a Counsellor of good things, and a Comfort in Cares & Grief.

{100} Wisdom cannot be had but from God
[8:10, 12-13] For Her sake I shall have estimation among the Multitude, and Honour with the Elders, [though I be young.]

When I hold my tongue they shall bide my leisure, and when I speak they shall give good ear unto me: if I talk much, they shall lay their hands upon their Mouth.

Moreover, by the meanes of her, I shall obtain immortality, and leave behind me an everlasting memorial to them that come after me

[8:16] [After I am come into mine house,] I will repose myself with her: for her Conversation hath no bitterness, and to live with her, hath no Sorrow, but Mirth and Joy.

{101} Chap. 8, 9 Without Wisdom the best man is nothing worth

[8:17-18] Now when I considered these things in myself, And pondered them in mine heart, how that to be allied unto Wisdom, is Immortality,

[And great pleasure it is to haue her friendship,] And in the works of her hands are infinite Riches, and in the exercise of conference with Her, prudence: and in Talking with Her a good Report: I went about seeking How to take Her to me.

[8:21] And when I perceived that I could not otherwise obtain Her, except God gave her me (and that was a point of Wisdom also to know whose Gift she was) I prayed unto the Lord, and besought him, and with my whole Heart I said:

{102} Neither can he tell how to please God

[9:1-2, 4-5] O God of my Fathers, and Lord of Mercy, Who hast made all Things with Thy Word,

And ordained Man through thy Wisdom, that he should have dominion over the Creatures, which Thou hast made,

Give me wisdom that Sitteth by Thy Throne, and reject me not from among thy Children:

For I Thy Servant and Son of Thy Handmaid, am a feeble person, and of a short Time, [and too young for the understanding of judgement and laws.]

[9:13-14] For what man is he that can know the Council of God? or who can think what the Will of the Lord is?

For the Thoughts of Mortal Men are Miserable, And our devices are but uncertain.

{103} Chap 9th A prayer unto God, for his wisdom

[9:15-17] For the Corruptible Body presseth down the Soul, and the Earthy Tabernacle weigheth down the Mind t,hat museth upon many Things.

And hardly do we guess aright at Things that are upon Earth, and with Labour doe we find the Things that are before us: But the Things that are in Heaven, who hath searched out?

And Thy Council who hath known, except Thou give Wisdom, and send Thy Holy Spirit from Above?

[9:9] Wisdom was with Thee: which knoweth Thy Works, and was present when Thou Madest the World, and knew what was acceptable in Thy Sight, and Right in....

{104} A prayer for Wisdom
[9:9-10].....Thy Commandments.

O send her out of thy Holy Heavens, and from the Throne of Thy Glory, that being present She may Labour with me, that I may know what is pleasing unto Thee.

[11:20, 22-23] [Yea and without these might they have fallen down with one blast, being persecuted of vengeance, and scattered abroad thorough the breath of thy power, but] Thou hast ordered all Things in Measure, and Number, and Weight.
For the whole world before Thee is as a little Grain of the Ballance, Yea as a drop of the morning dew that falleth down upon the Earth.

But Thou hast Mercy upon all: for Thou canst doe all things, and winkest at the Sins of men: because they should amend.

{105} Chap 11 God is Merciful to All

[11:24] For Thou lovest all the Things that are, and Abhorrest Nothing which Thou hast made: For never wouldst Thou have made any thing, if Thou hadst Hated it.

[[Solomon was not a predestinarian]]

[11:25] And how could any thing have endured if it had not been Thy will? or been preserved, if not called by Thee?

[[Nor seems to believe the fall of Adam]]

[11:26] But thou sparest all: for they are thine, O Lord, thou lover of souls.

(Our Church says, Every person Born into the World, deserves God's Wrath, and damnation. Article 9, Of Original or Birth Sin)

Lord C here breaks off for a while from his reading of the Wisdom of Solomon. He notes the author's belief that God loves all that he has made and believes there is a tension with the doctrine of predestination. Though (as far as we know) Lord C remained a member of the Anglican church, he was close to those (mainly in the non-conformist congregations) who believed – after Locke - that God-directed reason was the surest guide when determining truth, and that doctrinal constraints were neither necessary nor beneficial.

Lord C also seemed to think that the author was also questioning the Fall. This is probably not so, given the author's commitment to his Jewish heritage. We don't know whether Lord C had read Locke's The Reasonableness of Christianity, *but the ideas there were implicit in his* An Essay Concerning Human Understanding, *which is quoted extensively in this collection. Locke didn't deny the Fall, but he chose to ignore it.*

Lord C goes on to look at the references to the Fall and predestination in the Articles of the Church of England – the sixteenth century summary of the Church of England's position on Christian teaching.

{106} Articles of the Church of England
Article 11, Of the Justification of Men
We are accounted Righteous before God, only by the Merit of our Lord and Saviour Jesus Christ by Faith, and not for our own Works or Deservings: Wherefore, that we are Justified by Faith only is a most Wholesome Doctrine, and very full of Comfort [[for a Wicked Man]]. [[I think there is more Comfort in the Doctrine of Solomon]][135] .

---

[135] Lord C here clearly follows Locke, but it is interesting that these comments are the first he has

Article 17, Of Predestination and Election
Predestination to Life is the Everlasting purpose of God, whereby (before the Foundations of the World were laid) He hath constantly decreed by his Counsel secret to us,[[how do you know it then]] to deliver from curse and damnation [[the worst of mankind]] Those whom he has Chosen in Christ out of Mankind, and to bring them by Christ to...

{107} Articles of the Church of England
... to Everlasting Salvation, as Vessels made to Honour. Wherefore, they which He endued, with so excellent a Benefit of God, He called according to God's purpose by his Spirit working in due season: they through Grace obey the calling: they be justified freely: they be made sons of God by adoption: they be made like the image of his only-begotten Son Jesus Christ

[[God forbid that they should be like Him]]

They walk religiously in good works, [[not Always]]

and at last, by God's Mercy, they attain to Everlasting Felicity. [[Calvin, I don't Believe You]][136]

---

inserted, after a hundred pages of uncommented-on quotations.

[136] Article 17 is an exposition of the doctrine of

{108} Blank

{109} Wisdom of Solomon Chap. 13

[1-19] Surely vain are all Men by Nature, who are ignorant of God, and could not, out of the good things that are seen, know Him that is: neither by considering the Works did they acknowledge the Work-Master;

But deemed either Fire, or Wind, or the Swift Air, or the Circle of the Stars, or the Violent Water, or the Lights of Heaven, to be the Gods which Govern the World.

With whose Beauty, if they being delighted, took them to be Gods; let them know how much better the Lord of them is: for the first Author of Beauty hath Created Them.

{110} They were not to be excused that worshipped any of God's Works

---

predestination, which attempts to show that we find peace with God, not by 'being good' but by his freely given grace. I'm not clear why Lord C is so upset by it, unless he thinks the article suggests that some are predestined to be damned, which is not asserted here, and is believed by almost no mainstream Christians.

But if they were astonished at their power and virtue, let them understand by them, How much Mightier He is that made them.

For by the Greatness and Beauty of the Creatures, proportionably the Maker of them is seen.

But yet for this they are the less to be blamed; for They peradventure, were seeking God, and desirous to find Him[137].

For being Conversant in His works They search Him diligently, and believe their Sight: because the Things are Beautiful that are seen.

Howbeit, neither are they to be pardoned.

{111) But most wretched are They that worship the work of men's hands
For if They were able to know so much, that they could aim at the World; How did they not sooner find out the Lord thereof?

---

[137] The text of the KJV renders 'They peradventure err, seeking God, and desirous...' Lord C, intentionally or not, has presented a different (but quite reasonable) alternative version. A modern translation of the verse is 'Yet these people are little to be blamed, for perhaps they go astray while seeking God and desiring to find him'.

But Miserable are They, and in dead Things is their Hope, who call them gods, which are the works of Men's Hands, Gold and Silver, to shew Art in, and resemblances of Beasts, or a Stone good for nothing, the Work of an Ancient Hand.

Now a Carpenter that felleth Timber, after he hath sawn down a Tree meet for the purpose, and taken off all the Bark skilfully round about, and hath wrought it handsomely, and made a vessel thereof...

{112}
...[fit] for the service of Man's Life;

And after spending the refuse of his work to dress his Meat, hath filled Himself;

And taking the very refuse among those which served to no use (being a crooked piece of wood, and full of knots) hath carved it diligently, when he had nothing else to do, and formed it by the skill of his Understanding, and Fashioned it to the Image of a Man;

Or made it like some vile Beast, laying it over with Vermilion, and with paint colouring it Red, and covering every Spot therein;

And when he had made a convenient Room for it, set it in a Wall, and made it fast with Iron:

{113} The Folly of worshipping Idols
For He provided for it that it might not Fall, knowing that it was unable to help itself; for it is an image, and hath need of help:

Then maketh he prayer for his Goods, for his Wife and Children, and is not ashamed to speak to that which hath no Life.

For Health he calleth upon that which is weak: for Life prayeth to That which is dead; For Aid humbly beseecheth that which hath least means to help: and for a Good Journey he asketh of That which cannot set a Foot forward:

And for Gaining and Getting, and for good success of his Hands, asketh ability to do of Him, that is most unable to do any thing.

{114) They are saved by their Ships, Chap 14
[1-5] Again, one preparing himself to Sail, and about to pass through the raging Waves, calleth upon a piece of Wood more rotten than the Vessel that carrieth Him.

For verily desire of Gain devised Ships [[or Vessels]][138], and the Workman built it by his skill.

---

[138] The KJV has 'devised that'. Lord C seems to have decided that the sense was unclear and so substituted 'Ships or Vessels'.

But Thy providence, O Father, Governeth it: For Thou hast made a Way in the Sea, and a safe path in the Waves;

Shewing that Thou canst save from all danger: Yea, tho a Man went to Sea without Art.

Nevertheless thou wouldst not that the Works of Thy Wisdom should be Idle, and therefore do Men commit their Lives to a small piece of Wood, and passing the Rough Sea in a weak Vessel are saved.

{115} Chap. 14 The Beginning of Idolatry
[12-31] For the devising of Idols was the beginning of Spiritual Fornication, and the Invention of Them, the Corruption of Life

For neither were they from the beginning, neither shall they be for ever.

For by the vain glory of Men they entered into the World, and therefore shall they come shortly to an End.

For a father afflicted with Untimely Mourning, when He hath made an Image of his Child, soon taken away, now Honoured him as a God, which was then a dead Man, and delivered to Those that were under Him, Ceremonies and Sacrifices.

{116} The Rise of Odolatry
Thus in process of Time an ungodly Custom, grown strong, was kept as a Law, and Graven Images were Worshipped by the Commandments of Kings.

Whom Men could not Honour in presence, Because they dwelt far off, They took the Counterfeit of His visage from Far, and made an express Image of a King whom they Honoured, to the end that by This their forwardness, they might flatter Him that was absent, as if He were present.

Also, the singular diligence of the Artificer did help to set forward the Ignorant to more Superstition.

{117} Chap 14 The rise & the Effect of Idolatry
For the Artificer, willing to please one in Authority, forced all his Skill to make the resemblance, of the best fashion.

And so the Multitude, allured by the Grace of the Work, Took Him now for a God, which a little before was but [but] Honoured [[as a Man]][139].

---

[139] Lord C adds 'as a Man' to make the meaning clearer, as also, in the following verse, he adds 'of God'.

And this was an occasion to deceive the World: For Men, serving either Calamity or Tyranny, did ascribe unto Stones and Stocks the Incommunicable Name [[of God]].

Moreover, this was not enough for them, that they erred in the Knowledge of God; but [whereas they lived in the great war of ignorance, those so great plagues called they peace.

For whilst] They slew their Children in Sacrifices, [or used secret ceremonies, or made revellings of strange rites;

And kept neither Lives nor Marriages any longer undefiled: but either one Slew another traiterously, or Grieved Him by Adultery.

{118} The Effect of Idolatry – God will punish those that swear falsely by their Idols
Disquieting of good men, forgetfulness of good turns[140], So that there reigned in all Men without exception, Blood, Man Slaughter, Theft and Dissimulation, Corruption, unfaithfulness, Tumults, perjury,

---

[140] In the KJV, 'Disquieting of Good Men, forgetfulness of good turns' belongs to the following verse

[defiling of souls, changing of kind, disorder in marriages, adultery, and shameless uncleanness.

For the worshipping of idols not to be named is the beginning, the cause, and the end, of all evil.

For either they are mad when they be merry, or prophesy lies, or live unjustly, or else lightly forswear themselves.]

For insomuch as their Trust is in Idols, which have no life; Though they swear falsely, yet they look not to be hurt.

Howbeit for bot Causes shall they be justly punished; Both because they thought not well of God, giving heed unto Idols, and also unjustly swore in deceit, despising Holiness.

For it is not the power of them by whom they swear: But it is the just Vengeance of Sinners, that punisheth always the Offence of the Ungodly.

{119} Chap 15 We do Acknowledge the True God

[1-12] But thou, O God, art Gracious and true, longsuffering, and in Mercy ordering all Things,

[For if we sin, we are thine, knowing thy power: but we will not sin, knowing that we are counted thine.][141]

For to know Thee is perfect Righteousness: Yea, to know Thy power is the root of Immortality.

For neither did the Mischievous invention of Men deceive us, nor an Image spotted with divers Colours, the painter's fruitless Labour;

[the sight whereof enticeth fools to lust after it, and so they desire the form of a dead image, that hath no breath.]

Both They that make them, they that desire them, and They that worship them, are lovers of Evil Things, and are worthy to have such Things to Trust upon.

For the potter, tempering soft earth, fashioneth every vessel, with much labour for our service: [yea, of the same clay he maketh both the vessels that serve for clean uses, and likewise also all such as serve to the contrary: but what is the use of either sort, the potter himself is the judge.]

---

[141] Lord C omits this verse. He objects to any suggestion that – saved or unsaved – we do not sin.

And employing his labours lewdly, he maketh a vain God of the same

{120}
Clay, even He which a little before was made of the same Earth Himself, and within a little while after returneth to the same out of which he was taken, when His Life which was lent Him, shall be demanded.

Notwithstanding his care is, not [that he shall have much labour, nor] that his life is Short: but striveth to excel Goldsmiths and Silversmiths, and endeavoureth to do like the Workers in Brass, and counteth it his Glory to make counterfeit Things.

[His heart is ashes, his hope is more vile than earth, and his life of less value than clay:

Forasmuch as he knew not his Maker, and him that inspired into him an active soul, and breathed in a living spirit.

But] They counted our life a pastime, and our Time Here a Market for Gain: For, say they, We must be getting every way, though it be by Evil means.

{121} Chap 15 The Folly of Worshipping Idols

[16-17] For Man made Them, and He that borrowed his own Spirit fashioned them: but no Man can make a God like unto Himself.

[For being mortal, he worketh a dead thing with wicked hands:] For he himself is better than the Things which he worshippeth: Whereas he lived once, but They Never.

[16:13] [[But Thou O Lord]] hast power of Life and Death: thou leadest to the Gates of Hell, and bringest up again.

[16:15] And it is not possible to escape thine Hand

[17:11-12] For Wickedness, condemned by her own Witness, is very Timorous, and being pressed with Conscience, always forecasteth Grievous Things.

{122} Blank

The end of the Wisdom of Solomon – The beginning of Proverbs

{123} Blank

{124} Proverbs
[2:10-15] When Wisdom entereth into thine Heart, and Knowledge is pleasant unto thy Soul;

Discretion shall preserve Thee, Understanding shall keep Thee:

To deliver Thee from the way of the Evil Man, [from the man that speaketh froward things;

Who leave the paths of uprightness, to walk in the ways of darkness;

Who rejoice to do evil, *and* delight in the frowardness of the wicked;]

Whose Ways are Crooked, and They froward in their paths:

[3:3-5] Let not Mercy and Truth forsake Thee: bind them about thy Neck; Write them upon the Table of thine Heart:

So shalt Thou find Favour and good understanding in the Sight of God and Man.

Trust in the Lord with all thine Heart; and lean not unto thine own Understanding.

{125} Chap 2nd Proverbs
[3:13] Happy is the Man that findeth Wisdom, and the Man that getteth Understanding.

[3:16-17} Length of days is in her Right Hand; and in her left Hand Riches and Honour.

Her ways are ways of pleasantness, and all her paths are peace.

[3:23-24] Then shalt Thou Walk in thy way safely, and thy Foot shall not Stumble.

When thou liest down, thou shalt not be afraid: yea, thou shalt lie down, and thy Sleep shall be sweet.

[3:26-27] For the Lord shall be thy Confidence, and shall keep thy Foot from being taken.

Withhold not good from them to whom it is due, when it is in the power of thine Hand to do it.

{126} Chap 9th
[3:30-31] Strive not with a Man without Cause, if he have done thee no harm.

Envy thou not the Oppressor, and choose none of his Ways.

[4:23] Keep thy Heart with all diligence; for out of it are the Issues of life.

[9:7-10] He that reproveth a Scorner getteth to himself Shame: and he that rebuketh a Wicked Man getteth himself a Blot.

Reprove not a Scorner, lest he hate Thee: Rebuke a Wise Man, and he will love thee.

Give Instruction to a Wise Man, and he will be yet Wiser: Teach a just Man, and he will increase in Learning.

{127} Chap. 11th Proverbs
[10:8-9a] The wise in heart will receive Commandments: but a prating Fool shall fall.

He that walketh uprightly walketh surely:

[11:3a] [[and]] the integrity of the upright shall guide them.

[11:2] When pride cometh, then cometh shame: But with the lowly is Wisdom.

[11:7] When a Wicked Man dieth, his expectation shall perish: and the Hope of Unjust Men perisheth.

[11:10] When it goeth well with the Righteous, the City rejoiceth: and when the Wicked perish, there is Shouting.

[11:8] The Righteous is delivered out of Trouble, and the Wicked cometh in his Stead.

{128} Chap 12.
[11:12-13] He that is void of Wisdom despiseth his Neighbour: But a Man of Understanding holdeth his peace.

A Talebearer revealeth Secrets: but he that is of a faithful Spirit, concealeth the Matter.

[11:27] He that diligently seeketh Good, procureth favour: But he that seeketh Mischief, it shall come unto Him.

[11:29] He that troubleth his own House shall inherit the wind: and the Fool shall be servant to the wise of heart.

[12:8] A Man shall be commended according to his Wisdom: But he that is of a perverse heart shall be despised.

{129} Chap 12. Proverbs

[12:25] Heaviness in the Heart of Man maketh it stoop: but a good Word maketh it glad.

[12:15] The way of a Fool is right in his own Eyes: But he that hearkeneth unto Counsel is Wise.

[12:18-21] There is that speaketh like the piercings of a Sword: but the Tongue of the Wise is Health.

The lip of Truth shall be established for ever: But a lying Tongue is but for a Moment.

Deceit is in the Heart of them that imagine Evil: But to the counsellors of peace is Joy.

There shall no Evil happen to the Just: But the wicked shall be filled with Mischief.

{130} Chap 13.
[12:24] The Hand of the Diligent shall bear Rule: but the slothful shall be under Tribute.

[13:3-4] He that keepeth his Mouth keepeth his Life: For He that openeth wide his Lips shall have destruction.

The Soul of the Sluggard desireth, and hath nothing: but the Soul of the Diligent shall be made fat.

[13:6] Righteousness keepeth him that is upright in the way: but Wickedness overthroweth the Sinner.

[13:12] Hope deferred maketh the Heart Sick: but when the desire cometh, it is a Tree of Life.

[13:19a] The desire accomplished is sweet to the Soul:

{131} Chap 14. Proverbs
[13:20] He that walketh with Wise Men, shall be Wise: but a Companion of Fools shall be destroyed.

[14:7] Go from the presence of a Foolish Man, when Thou perceivest not in him the Sign of Knowledge[142].

---

142 The KJV has 'the lips of knowledge'.

[14:9a] Fools make a mock at Sin:

[16:25] [[and]] there is a way that seemeth right to a Man, but the end thereof are the ways of Death.

[14:13] Even in Laughter the Heart is sorrowful; And the end of that Mirth is Heaviness

[14:16] A wise Man feareth, and departeth from Evil: but the Fool rageth, and is Confident.

{132} Chap 15.
[14:15] The Simple believeth every Word: but the prudent Man looketh well to his going.

[14:17] He that is soon Angry dealeth Foolishly: and a Man of Wicked Devices is Hated.

[14:20] The poor is hated even of his own neighbour: but the rich hath many friends.

[15:1] A soft Answer turneth away Wrath: but Grievous Words stir up Anger.

[15:13] A Merry Heart maketh a Cheerful Countenance: But by Sorrow of the Heart the Spirit is broken.

[15:15] All the Days of the Afflicted are Evil: But he that is of a Merry Heart, hath a constant Feast.

{133} Chap 15. Proverbs

[15:16-18] Better is little with the Fear of the Lord , than great Treasure and trouble therewith.

Better is a Dinner of Herbs where Love is, than a Stalled Ox and Hatred therewith.

A wrathful man stirreth up Strife: but he that is slow to Anger appeaseth Strife.

[15:22] Without Counsel purposes are disappointed: but in the multitude of Counsellors they are established.

[15:23b] A word spoken in due Season, how good is it!

[15:28] The Heart of the Righteous studieth to answer: But the Mouth of the Wicked poureth out Evil Things.

{134} Chap 16.
[15:30] The light of the Eyes rejoiceth the Heart: And a good Report maketh the Bones Fat.

[16:1] The preparations of the Heart in Man, and the Answer of the Tongue, is from the Lord.

[16:3] Commit thy Works unto the Lord, and thy Thoughts shall be established.

[16:7] When a Man's Ways please the Lord, He maketh even his Enemies to be at peace with Him.

[16:24] Pleasant Words are as an Honey-comb, Sweet to the Soul, and Health to the Bones.

[16:27] An Ungodly Man, diggeth up Evil: and in his lips there is as a Burning Fire.

{135} Chap 17.
[16:28-29] A Froward Man soweth strife: and a Whisperer separateth chief Friends.

A violent Man enticeth his Neighbour, and leadeth him into the way that is not Good.

[16:32] He that is slow to Anger is better than the Mighty; And he that ruleth his Spirit than he that taketh a City.

[17:10] A reproof entereth more into a wise Man than an Hundred Stripes into a Fool.

[17:12-13] Let a Bear robbed of her Whelps meet a Man, rather than a Fool in his Folly.

Whoso rewardeth Evil for Good, Evil shall not depart from His House.

{136} Proverbs

[17:14-15] The beginning of Strife is as when one letteth out Water: Therefore leave off Contention, before it be meddled with.

He that Justifieth the Wicked, and he that Condemneth the Just, even they both are an Abomination to the Lord.

[17:17] A Friend loveth at all times, and a Brother is born for Adversity.

[17:19a] He loveth Transgression that loveth strife:

[17:20b-21] and he that hath a perverse Tongue falleth into Mischief.

He that begetteth a Fool doeth it to his Sorrow: and the Father of a Fool hath no Joy.

{137} Chap 18. Proverbs

[16:20a] He that handleth a matter wisely shall find good:

[16:22b] but the instruction of fools is folly.

[16:18] Pride goeth before Destruction, and an Haughty Spirit before a Fall.

[17:27a] He that hath Knowledge spareth his Words:

[17:28] Even a Fool, when he holdeth his peace, is counted Wise: and he that shutteth his Lips is esteemed a Man of Understanding.

[18:3] When the Wicked cometh, then cometh also Contempt, and with ignominy reproach.

[18:6a] A fool's lips enter into contention,

[18:7a] and his tongue is his destruction.[143]

{138}
[18:8a] The Words of a Talebearer are as Wounds,

[18:21} [[and]] Death and Life are in the power of the Tongue:

[18:14] The Spirit of a Man will sustain his Infirmity; But a wounded Spirit who can bear.

[18:13] He that answereth a Matter before he heareth it, it is Folly and shame unto him.

[18:17] He that is first in his Own Cause seemeth Just; but his Neighbour cometh and searcheth Him.

---

[143] Lord C has combined the first half of 18:6 with the first half of 18:7, though the KJV has 'A fool's mouth is hid destruction'. I imagine he thought 'tongue' carried the meaning better. 'Mouth' seems to gave been scrubbed out in his text.

[18:19] A Brother offended is harder to be won than a strong City: and their Contentions are like the Bars of a Castle.

{139} Chap. 19. Proverbs
[18:23] The poor useth intreaties; but the Rich[[man]] answereth Roughly.

[19:1] Better is the poor that walketh in his Integrity, than he that is perverse in his Lips, and is a Fool.

[19:3-6] The Foolishness of Man perverteth his Ways: and his Heart fretteth against the Lord.

Wealth maketh many Friends; but the poor is separated from his Neighbour.

A False Witness shall not be unpunished, and he that speaketh Lies shall not escape.

Many will intreat the favour of the Rich[144]: and every Man is a Friend to him that giveth Gifts.

{140}
[19:7-8] All the Brethren of the poor do Hate him: How much more do his Friends go far from Him? he pursueth them with Words, Yet they are wanting to him.

---

[144] The KJV has ‘intreat the favour of the prince’.

He that getteth Wisdom loveth his own Soul: He that findeth understanding shall find Good.

[19:11] The Discretion of a Man deferreth his Anger; And it is his Glory to pass over a Transgression.

[19:15] Slothfulness casteth into a Deep Sleep; and an Idle Soul shall suffer Hunger.

[19:24] A slothful Man hideth his hand in his Bosom, and will not so much as bring it to his Mouth again.

{141} Chap. 20. Proverbs

[20:3] It is an Honour for a Man to cease from Strife: But every Fool will be meddling.

[20:6] Most Men will proclaim every one his own Goodness: But a faithful Man who can find.

[20:9] Who can say, I have made my heart clean, I am pure from my Sin?

[20:14] It is naught, it is naught, saith the buyer: but when he is gone his way, then he boasteth.

[20:17] Bread of deceit is sweet to a Man; but afterwards his Mouth shall be filled with Gravel.

[20:19] He that goeth about as a Talebearer, revealeth Secrets: therefore meddle not with him that flattereth with his Lips.

{142} Chap 21
[20:21-22] An Inheritance may be gotten hastily at the beginning; but the end thereof shall not be Blessed.

Say not Thou, I will recompense Evil; But wait on the Lord, and he shall save Thee.

[21:6-7] The getting of Treasures by a lying Tongue is a vanity tossed to and fro of them that seek death.

The Robbery of the Wicked shall destroy them; Because they refuse to do Judgment.

[21:10] The Soul of the Wicked desireth Evil: his Neighbour findeth no favour in his Eyes.

[21:14] A Gift in Secret pacifieth Anger: and a reward in the Bosom strong Wrath.

{142}[145] Chap 21. Proverbs
[21:17] He that loveth pleasure shall be a poor Man: He that loveth Wine and Oil shall not be Rich.

[21:16] The Man that wandereth out of the way of Understanding, Shall remain in the Congregation of the Dead.

---

[145] Lord C has marked two pages '142'

[21:19] It is better to dwell in the Wilderness, than with a Contentious and an Angry Man[146].

[21:21] He that followeth after Righteousness and Mercy, Findeth Life, Righteousness, and Honour.

[21:23] Whoso keepeth his Mouth and his Tongue keepeth his Soul from Troubles.

{143} Chap 22

[21:25-26a] The Desire of the Slothful killeth Him; He Coveteth greedily all the day long:

But his Hands refuse to Labour.

[22:1-4] A Good Name is rather to be chosen than great Riches, and loving Favour rather than Silver and Gold.

The Rich and poor meet together: the Lord is the Maker of them all.

---

[146] The KJV has 'an angry woman'. This is not first time that Lord C has changed the specific word 'woman' for (what was then) the more gender neutral term 'man', meaning person. He resists speaking slightingly of women. It would be pleasant to think that these notebooks come from the last six years of his life, when he had found happiness with Jane Davis.

A prudent Man foreseeth the Evil, and hideth himself: But the Simple pass on, and are punished.

By Humility and the Fear of the Lord are Riches, and Honour, and Life.

{144} Chap 22. Proverbs
[22:5] Thorns and Snares are in the way of the froward: He that doth keep his Soul shall be far from them.

[22:7-8] The Rich ruleth over the poor, and the Borrower is Servant to the Lender.

He that soweth iniquity shall reap vanity: and the Rod of his Anger shall fail.

[22:10] Cast out the Scorner, and Contention shall go out; Yea, strife and reproach shall Cease.

[22:22-23] Rob not the poor, because he is poor: neither oppress the Afflicted [in the gate]:

For the Lord will plead their Cause, and spoil the Soul of those that spoiled them.

{145}
[22:24-25] Make no Friendship with an Angry Man; and with a furious Man thou shalt not go:

Lest Thou [learn his ways, and] get a snare to thy Soul.

[22:26-27] Be not Thou one of them that strike hands, or of them that are Sureties for Debts.

If thou hast nothing to pay, Why should he take away thy Bed from Under Thee?

[22:29] Seest thou a Man diligent in his Business? he shall stand before Kings; he shall not stand before mean Men.

[23:1-2] When thou sittest to eat with a Ruler, consider diligently what is before thee:

And put a Knife to thy Throat, if thou be a Man given to Appetite.

{146} Chap 23. About avoiding Quarrels

[23:4-7] Labour not to be Rich: Cease from thine own Wisdom.

Wilt thou set thine Eyes upon that which is not? For Riches certainly make themselves Wings; they fly away as an Eagle toward Heaven.

Eat thou not the Bread of him that hath an Evil Eye, neither desire thou his dainty Meats:

For as he thinketh in his Heart, so is he: Eat and Drink, saith he to thee; but his heart is not with Thee.

[23:9] Speak not in the ears of a Fool: for he will despise the Wisdom of thy Words.

{147} And sundry Causes thereof. Chap 24
[24:10] If thou faint in the day of adversity, thy strength is small.

[24:12] If Thou sayest, Behold, we knew it not; doth not he that pondereth the Heart consider it? and He that keepeth thy Soul, doth not He know it? and shall not he render to every Man according to his Works?

[24:17-20] Rejoice not when thine Enemy falleth, and let not thine heart be glad when he Stumbleth:

Lest the Lord see it, and it displease Him, and He turn away his Wrath from him.

Fret not thyself because of Evil Men, neither be thou Envious at the Wicked:

For there shall be no reward to the Evil Man; the Candle of the Wicked shall be put out.

{148} Chap 24. About Contentious busy-bodies...
[24:21-22a] My Son, fear thou the LORD and the king: and meddle not with them that are given to Change:

For their Calamity shall rise suddenly;

[24:29] Say not, I will do so to him as he hath done to me: I will render to the Man according to his Work. [[But put Thy Trust in the Lord]][147]

[24:24-26] He that saith unto the Wicked, Thou are Righteous; Him shall the people Curse, Nations shall abhor Him:

But to them that rebuke him shall be delight, and a Blessing shall come upon Him.

Every Man shall Kiss his Lips that giveth a right answer.

[25:11] A Word fitly spoken is like Apples of Gold in pictures of Silver.

{149} ...and Fools & false Friends

[25:18-22] A Man that beareth false Witness against his Neighbour is [a maul, and] a Sword, and a Sharp Arrow.

Confidence in an unfaithful Man in time of Trouble is like a broken Tooth, and a Foot out of Joint.

As he that taketh away a Garment in Cold Weather, And as Vinegar upon Nitre, so is he that singeth Songs to an heavy Heart.

---

[147] This appears to be Lord C's own addition, though in keeping with the sense of the text

If thine Enemy be Hungry, give him Bread to Eat; and if he be thirsty, give him Water to drink:

[For thou shalt heap coals of fire upon his head,] and the Lord shall reward thee.

[25:28] He that hath no rule over his own Spirit is like a City that is broken down, and without Walls.

{150} Chap 26. Observations about Contentions and Busy-bodies...

[26:17] He that passeth by, and meddleth with Strife belonging not to him, is like one that taketh a Dog by the Ears.

[26:20-23] Where no Wood is, there the Fire goeth out: So where there is no talebearer, the strife ceaseth.

As Coals are to Burning Coals, and Wood to Fire; so is a Contentious man to kindle Strife.

The Words of a Talebearer are as Wounds, and go down into the Heart[148].

---

[148] The KJV has 'and they go down into the innermost parts of the belly'. Lord C (characteristically) prefers to avoid too much anatomy, though the imagery is less apt.

Burning lips and a Wicked heart, are like a potsherd covered with Silver Dross.

[26:28] A lying Tongue hateth those that are afflicted by it; And a flattering mouth worketh ruin.

{151} ...and Fools and Hypocrites
[26:24-27] He that Hateth Dissembleth with his lips, and layeth up Deceit within him.

When he speaketh fair, believe him not: for there are seven Abominations in his Heart.

Whose Hatred is covered by Deceit, his wickedness shall be shewed before the whole Congregation.

Whoso diggeth a pit shall fall therein: and he that rolleth a Stone, it will return upon him.

[27:6] Faithful are the Wounds of a Friend; but the Kisses of an Enemy are Deceitful.

[27:3] A Stone is Heavy, and the Sand Weighty; but a Fool's Wrath is heavier than them both.

[29:12] If a Ruler hearken to Lies, All his servants are wicked. Chap 29, verse 12.

{152} Chap 27. The Happiness of a Friend
[27:9] Ointment and perfume rejoice the Heart: so doth the Sweetness of a Man's Friend by hearty Counsel.

[27:17] Iron sharpeneth Iron; so a Man sharpeneth the Counsel[149] of his Friend.

[27:10] Thine own Friend, and thy Father's Friend, forsake not; [neither go into thy brother's house] for in the day of thy calamity better is such a one, than a Brother[150].

[28:4] They that forsake the Law praise the Wicked: But such as keep the Law contend with them.

[28:11] The rich Man is Wise in his own Conceit; but the poor that hath Understanding searcheth him out.

{153} Against Anger, and Flattery Proverbs
[28:21] To have respect of persons is not Good: for, for a piece of Bread that Man will Transgress.

[29:5] A Man that flattereth his Neighbour spreadeth a Net for his Feet.

[29:9] If a Wise Man contendeth with a Foolish Man, whether he Rage or Laugh, there is no Rest.

---

[149] The KJV has 'the countenance of a friend'.
[150] The KJV has 'better is a neighbour that is near than a brother far off'.

[29:20] Seest thou a Man that is hasty in his Words? There is more hope of a Fool than of Him.

[29:25] The Fear of Man bringeth a Snare: but whoso putteth his Trust in the Lord, shall be safe.

[29:22] An Angry Man stirreth up Strife, and a furious Man aboundeth in Transgression.

[29:27] An Unjust Man is an Abomination to the Just: and He that is upright in the Way is an Abomination to the Wicked.

{154} Chap 30 Proverbs

[30:7] Two things have I required of Thee; deny me them not before I die:

[30:8-9] Remove far from me Vanity and Lies: give me neither poverty nor Riches; feed me with food convenient for me:

Lest I be full, and deny Thee, and say, Who is the Lord? or lest I be poor, and Steal, and take the Name of my God in Vain.

[30:6] Add [thou] not unto his Words, lest he reprove Thee, and thou be found a Liar

[29:8] Scornful Men bring a City into a Snare: but Wise Men turn away Wrath.

[29:11] A Fool uttereth all his Mind: but a Wise Man keepeth it in till Afterwards.

The End of Proverbs. The Beginning of Ecclesiastes

{155} Ecclesiastes All Human Courses are Vain

[1:2-4a] Vanity of Vanities, says the preacher [vanity of vanities] all is vanity.

What profit hath a Man of all his Labours which he taketh under the Sun?

One Generation passeth away, and another Generation cometh:

[1:9-11] The thing that hath been, it is that which shall be; [and that which is done is that which shall be done:] and there is no new thing under the Sun.

Is there any thing whereof it may be said, See, this is New? it hath been already of old time, which was before us.

There is no remembrance of former Things; neither shall there be any remembrance of Things that are to come, with those that shall come after.

{156} Chap 2nd

[1:12-15a] I the Preacher was King over Israel in Jerusalem.

And I gave my heart to seek and search out, by Wisdom, concerning all Things that are done under Heaven: [this sore travail hath God given to the sons of man to be exercised therewith.]

I have seen all the Works that are done under the Sun; and, behold, all is Vanity and Vexation of Spirit.

That which is Crooked cannot be made straight:

[1:17-18] And I gave my Heart to know Wisdom, [[and to know Wisdom]] and to know Madness and Folly: I perceived that this also is Vexation of Spirit.

For in much Wisdom is much Grief: and he that increaseth Knowledge increaseth Sorrow.

{157] The Vanity of Human Courses in the way of pleasure

[2:1-4] I said in mine heart, Go to now, I will prove thee with Mirth, therefore enjoy pleasure: And, Behold, this also is Vanity.

I said of Laughter, it is Mad: and of Wirth, What doeth it?

I sought in mine heart to give myself unto Wine, [yet acquainting mine heart with wisdom;] and to lay hold on Folly, till I might see, what was that good for the Sons of Men, which they should do under the Heaven all the Days of their Life.

I made me great works; I Builded me Houses; I planted me Vineyards:

[2:10] And what[soever] mine Eyes desired I kept not from them, I withheld not my heart from any Joy; for my heart rejoiced in all my Labour: and this was my portion of all my Labour.

{158} Chap. 2nd Ecclesiastes
[2:12-14a] And I turned myself to behold Wisdom, and Madness, and Folly: [for what can the man do that cometh after the king? even that which hath been already done.]

Then I saw that Wisdom excelleth Folly, as far as light excelleth darkness.

The Wise Man's Eyes are in his Head; But the fool walketh in darkness:

[2:16] For there is no remembrance of the Wise more than of the Fool for Ever;[seeing that which now is in the days to come shall all be forgotten.] And how dieth the Wise Man? as the Fool.

[2:15b] Then I said in my heart, that this also is vanity.

[2:17-18a] Therefore I Hated Life; [because the work that is wrought under the sun is grievous unto me:] for all is Vanity and Vexation of Spirit.

Yea, I Hated all my Labour which I had taken under the Sun: because I should...

{159} the Vanity of Human Labour

[2:18b] ....leave it unto the man that shall be after me.

[2:19]And who knoweth whether he shall be a Wise Man or a Fool? [yet] He shall have Rule over all my Labour [wherein I have laboured, and wherein I have shewed myself wise under the sun.] This also is vanity.

[2:22-24] [For] What hath Man of all his Labour, and of the Vexation of his heart, [wherein he hath laboured under the sun?]

For all his Days are Sorrows, and]his travail] Grief; And his Heart taketh not rest in the Night. This is also Vanity.

There is nothing better for a Man, than that he should eat and drink, and that he should make his Soul enjoy good in his labour. This also I saw [, that it was] from the Hand of God.

[2:26a] For God giveth to a Man that is Good in his sight.

{160} Ecclesiastes Chap 2.
[2:26a] For God giveth to a Man that is good in his Sight, Wisdom, and Knowledge, and Joy:

[3:17] I said in mine Heart, God shall Judge the Righteous and the Wicked: for there is a Time there for [every purpose and for] every work.

[3:21] Who knoweth the Spirit of a Man that goeth Upward, and the Spirit of a Beast that goeth downward to the Earth?

[3:20] All go unto one place; All are of the Dust, and all turn to Dust Again.

[3:22] Wherefore I perceive that there is nothing better, than that a Man should rejoice in his own Works; for that is his portion: For who shall bring him to see what shall be after Him?

{161}
[4:1-2] [So] I [returned, and] considered all the Oppressions that are done under the Sun: And behold the Tears of such as were oppressed, And they had no Comforter; [and on the side of their oppressors there was power; but they had no comforter.]

Wherefore I praised the Dead which are already dead more than the Living [which are yet alive].

[4:9-10] Two are better than one; [because they have a good reward for their labour.]

For if they fall, the one will lift up his fellow: But Woe to him that is alone when he falleth; [for he hath not another to help him up.]

{162} Blank

Here follows an index to the second & third notebooks – which suggests these were bound together in Lord Catherlough's lifetime.

www.ingramcontent.com/pod-product-compliance
Lightning Source LLC
LaVergne TN
LVHW012051160826
845678LV00014B/2779

9798423170110